SHERLOCK HOLMES

H.R.F. Keating

SHERLOCK HOLMES

The Man and His World

with 136 illustrations

CASTLE BOOKS

This edition published in 2006 by
Castle Books ®
A division of Book Sales, Inc.
114 Northfield Avenue
Edison, NJ 08837

This book is reprinted with permission of
Peters Fraser & Dunlop, London.

ISBN-13: 978-0-7858-2112-0
ISBN-10: 0-7858-2112-0

Printed in the United States of America

SHERLOCK HOLMES. His name is known at the furthest reaches of the earth. You can read of his exploits in Basuto. You can read of them in Eskimo. Yet we know extraordinarily little of the world's first and greatest consulting detective. He constantly expressed an unyielding dislike of the clammy hands of publicity, and there is no entry under 'Holmes, Sherlock' in all the sixty and more volumes of *The Dictionary of National Biography* nor among the thousands of obituaries in *The Times* is any record to be found even of the date of his death. We do not know when or where he was born.

Virtually our sole evidence of his existence comes in the accounts of a handful of his many cases as set out with grudging permission by his friend of long standing, his only friend indeed, Dr John H. Watson M.D. There have, of course, been suggestions and conjectures about his life ever since the Watson records came to an end, conjectures that now far exceed in bulk the whole total of the original accounts. But conjecture in biography is a sin as deplorable as simony in the Church (though perhaps more often committed) and it will be my endeavour in this portrayal of Sherlock Holmes and his world to avoid it.

So our account must start not with a birth but with a beginning. In or about the year 1873 young Sherlock Holmes investigated his first case, a mystery which Dr Watson was to chronicle many years later under the title 'The Gloria Scott'. Holmes was then a mere undergraduate, at either Oxford or Cambridge – Watson's necessarily discreet records never make it clear which – and it was to be some time before he exercised his already remarkable powers again.

But the date that saw this beginning was significant. England, of which Holmes was a native son if ever there was, at this period was also at a beginning. But it was the beginning of nothing so auspicious as the career about to open in front of that new phenomenon, the consulting detective. Britain at about the year 1870 was on the brink of a long slide-down from a position of true power and rare stability, a decline from an age of equipoise which has not ended more than a hundred years later.

She was then a nation at peace. Bar the one excrescence of the Crimean War, she had not been engaged in any major conflict for more than half a century. She was a nation of commerce. Her trade millions were well double those of Germany and France, her nearest rivals, put together. She was a nation of prestige. Not since Spain in the sixteenth century nor the France of the Sun King had any country so patently held the leadership of the world. She was a nation of quiet home-lovers, with an air from a now long-forgotten operetta, John Howard Payne's *Clari, the Maid of Milan*, almost her national anthem, so often was it warbled

Home, home, sweet, sweet home!
There's no place like home!
There's no place like home!

She was a religious nation. Family prayers were said each morning in houses great and small throughout the land. Sunday church-going was almost everywhere the rule and the day of rest was so consecrated that no entertainment, not even the modest dinner-party, not even the reading of fiction other than that of John Bunyan, was countenanced. 'Haste put your playthings all away, Tomorrow is the Sabbath Day,' the *Infants Magazine* admonished. And books on religion were in 1870 by far the largest class of new publications, 811 of them compared with 381 novels.

She was a nation of order. We see this still strongly enduring in the world in which Sherlock Holmes was to move. On many an occasion he requested the faithful Watson to turn up in *Bradshaw* a train to some country destination and off they hurried by cab certain that it would depart to the minute and arrive on time. He had only to put a letter into the post in the morning to be sure it would be delivered on the other side of London that evening. On one notable occasion when he received a coded message based on *Whitaker's Almanack* he was momentarily thrown because since it was 7 January he was, of course, using the new edition of that reference annual whereas his correspondent had been using the old. When, in investigating the case of the Three Students (in either Cambridge or Oxford), he took some wood chippings to each of the four stationers of any consequence in the town and discovered that they were from a pencil of an unusual size each shop at once assured him that they could immediately order a duplicate.

6

The pyramid of Victorian society which Sherlock Holmes's adventures took him up and down, down and up. Here that society is seen by George Cruikshank.

And, above all, Britain was a nation dedicated to work, to sober, earnest work. 'Work', said Thomas Carlyle, most thunderous of Victorian sages, addressing the students of Edinburgh University in 1866, 'is the grand cure of all the maladies and miseries that ever beset mankind.' Browning echoed him in his poem *Pacchiarotto and How He Worked in Distemper*

> *Man's work is to labour and leaven –*
> *As best he may – earth here with heaven;*
> *'Tis work for work's sake he's needing.*

Samuel Smiles.

And Samuel Smiles, author of that essence-of-the-period bestseller *Self-Help*, who coined the phrase which is the epitome of an ordered age, 'A place for everything and everything in its place', chimed in with 'In this necessity for exertion, we find the chief source of human advancement – the advancement of individuals as of nations. It has led to most of the mechanical inventions of the age. It has stimulated the shipbuilder, the merchant, the manufacturer, the machinist, the tradesman, the skilled workman.' While that magisterial art critic Ruskin contemplating Millais's *Mariana in the Moated Grange* pronounced, 'If the painter had painted Mariana *at work* in an unmoated grange . . . it would have been more to the purpose.'

Finally, Britain was a moral nation. Those were the days in which it was said, and very often truly said, that an Englishman's word was his bond. They were the days that Rudyard Kipling

Above all, Victorian Britain was a nation dedicated to work, described by Carlyle (seen here at the extreme right, in hat) in a famous address as 'the grand cure of all the maladies and miseries that ever beset mankind'. The painting *Work* is by Ford Madox Brown.

Right: Mariana, the painting by Millais inspired by Tennyson's poem. 'She said, I am aweary, aweary, I would that I were dead'. The picture drew Ruskin's condemnation. 'If the artist had painted Mariana *at work* . . .'

had in mind when he wrote, before Queen Victoria was dead, in his 'Song of the English':

Keep ye the Law – be swift in all obedience –
Clear the land of evil, drive the road and bridge the ford.
Make ye sure to each his own
That he reap where he hath sown;
By the peace among our peoples let men know we serve the Lord!

The whole was summed up in the notion, distinct if hard to define, of the English gentleman, hard to define perhaps because, as that lively Victorian Surtees, creator of the fox-hunting grocer Mr Jorrocks, said, 'The man who is always talking about being a gentleman never is one.' Indeed, a Victorian collection of useful sayings like *Ward's Prose Quotations* is reduced under the heading of 'gentleman' to giving only two or three instances and then saying, 'See Christianity, dress'. And Christianity certainly had a part in the creation of this mysterious entity. But so did dress. 'His dress and bearing', Dr Watson unhesitatingly declares, in his account of the Norwood Builder case, of a new client was 'that of a gentleman.' And in the Black Peter affair he states of a nocturnal capture, 'he was

Holmes and Watson capture an intruder 'dressed like a gentleman'. One of Sidney Paget's illustrations for Watson's account of the Black Peter affair.

dressed like a gentleman in Norfolk jacket and knickerbockers, with a cloth cap upon his head.' But Holmes himself has a higher standard. When at last he laid hands on the man who had stolen the Bruce-Partington submarine plans he rounded on him implacably with 'How an English gentleman could behave in such a manner is beyond my comprehension.'

Because, however concocted, the ideal of the English gentleman was a very real one and one by no means to be despised. It was impressed on the hearts and minds of men who by the thousand went out from their country and set an example to the world. In the end the ideal may not have been enough. But it was one to compare with that of the noble Roman or of the *chevalier sans peur et sans reproche*. It was looked up to, admired and imitated all over the globe, that strange, indefinable yet quite clear notion of always and in all circumstances 'doing the decent thing'.

It was an ideal embodied in the person of Mr Sherlock Holmes as if he had been created for this and no other purpose. 'I believe you are a man of your word and a white man,' an antagonist said to him late in his career. The turn of speech is outmoded now to the point of ridiculousness. Yet the thought behind it is not without validity even today.

But this picture of the era of equipoise is not, of course, the whole picture. On the glowing shine there were blemishes, and worse. In the fair blooming rose the worm of doubt was quietly gnawing. If Britain as a whole was boundingly prosperous, her very poor, the lowest of the low, lived in appalling squalor. If honesty was almost everywhere the keynote, in the crammed rookeries of the great cities it was each man for himself. There you found no church-goers, no Sunday observance. And if Tennyson, fresh from a first ride on the ever-spreading railways and under the delusion that the train wheels ran in slits, was optimistically proclaiming

> *Forward, forward let us range,*
> *Let the great world spin for ever down the ringing grooves of change*

Matthew Arnold was questioning in *The Scholar-Gipsy*:

> *What wears out the souls of mortal men?*
> *'Tis that from change to change their being rolls;*
> *'Tis that repeated shocks, again, again,*
> *Exhaust the energy of strongest souls.*

But the doubting was overwhelmed by the exuberant surface and poverty and vice were kept well behind the tall new

buildings that surrounded the fetid rookeries. All was well. Until somewhere about the year 1870.

Then or thereabouts the various earthquake tremors began that started to make the whole majestic fabric crumble. In 1870 on a fateful 4 August across on the far side of the safe barrier of the Channel sudden war flared out between France and Germany and in six short months the balance of power that had prevailed in Europe had gone. From now on Germany was the leader, the looked to, the admired. Her methods, smacking of the new sciences and high organization, opened up new possibilities to envious other nations and an arms race began that was not to reach its culmination until a 4 August forty-four years later. Abruptly Britain doubted her place and shouted her alarm.

Two years later, quite suddenly, the country launched itself on a new policy that was to have a tremendous impact all over the world and a profound one on the minds of its citizens at home. Until this time the Empire that Britain had acquired had been looked on as something of a liability, and a temporary liability at that. A senior Colonial Office civil servant even as late as 1871 wrote happily, 'I have always believed that the destiny of our colonies is independence.' But in the next year Disraeli, Leader of the Conservative Opposition, once equally lukewarm about what Dr Watson was to call 'our Indian possessions', and our African ones, declared in a speech at the Crystal Palace that the attempt to cast off these encumbrances had entirely failed. 'But how has it failed?' he asked. 'Through the sympathy of the Colonies for the Mother Country.' On this ground, he declared, Britain's policy must be to solidify this Empire, to invest in it morally. Imperialism stepped on to the grand stage. Soon it was to be the policy of the party in power.

That diamonds had been discovered some three years earlier at Kimberley in South Africa and that in Germany Prince Bismarck was rattling his sabre may have been other factors that brought about the change. But whatever its causes it was to be a mighty change and one that affected in countless ways, both grave and slight, the career of the young student of the sciences (at either Oxford or Cambridge) soon to give a first glimpse of his powers. Many of the most dangerous foes he was to encounter learnt their trade in the Colonies. Equally the Empire was to influence those trivial matters, which as he once pointed out can be so significant ('It is, of course, a trifle, but there is nothing so important as trifles'), such as the dish of strong-tasting curried mutton served to the stable-lads in the Silver Blaze case or the curried chicken presented to an early-morning guest during the

Opposite: London houses, as seen from a train by Gustave Doré. If Britain as a whole was boundingly prosperous in late Victorian times, her poor were often huddled in miserable conditions.

business of the Naval Treaty by a landlady who, though her cuisine was limited, 'has as good an idea of breakfast as a Scotch-woman'.

There were other developments in 1870 which had consequences as far-reaching and as disturbing. There was the passing of the Education Act which permitted compulsory schooling for every child among Britain's thirty-one million people. Less than twenty years later, during that same case of the Naval Treaty, Holmes was travelling back to London from Surrey sunk in profound thought about the complicated business he was engaged upon, when abruptly he looked up.

'It's a very cheering thing to come into London by any of these lines which run high and allow you to look down upon the houses like this,' he said.

Turning to the rows of sordid little homes beside the line, Watson thought his friend must be joking. But not at all.

'Look at those big, isolated clumps of building rising up above the slates, like brick islands in a lead-coloured sea.'

'The Board schools.'

'Lighthouses, my boy! Beacons of the future! Capsules, with hundreds of bright little seeds in each, out of which will spring

From the year 1872 onwards, Disraeli led the Conservative Party in a policy of Imperialism, a policy that came to a climax in 1876 when, on his advice, Queen Victoria assumed the title of Empress of India. *Punch's* view of the move.

'It is a very cheering thing to come into London by any of these lines which run high and allow you to look down upon the houses.' Not for the first time the paradoxical Holmes shocks Dr Watson before he points to the Board Schools, those 'beacons of the future' rising up above the slates. Paget's illustration for a conversation in 'The Naval Treaty'.

the wiser, better England of the future. I suppose that man Phelps does not drink?'

And Holmes, with one of those sudden switches of thought characteristic of the power he had over his mind, reverted to considering the immediate matter in hand.

So Watson had no opportunity to reflect on his friend's observations. But they show that pervasive optimism so typical of the Victorian era, though it was soon to be clouded by a hectically contrary strain, both in the times and in Holmes himself. The thoughts he voiced on this otherwise silent journey are one of his comparatively rare expressions of belief, and they show him as fundamentally at one with such giants of the age as Tennyson, ever ready to peal out optimism, and Carlyle, preacher, however precariously, of 'the everlasting Yea'.

And his views about these beacons of the future were to be justified in part in a curious way. By the time the bulk of Watson's accounts of his exploits was before the public there had been created out of the new prevailing literacy substantial upper layers of individuals able to comprehend ideas that had until this time generally been the preserve of the few. So that there were readers there waiting in numbers who were capable of

A telegraph exchange in 1871.

appreciating the scientific method, the method that was Holmes's great contribution to the business of the detection of crime. And these readers brought him that astonishing popularity which, often against his wishes, he came to acquire.

Yet it is to be doubted that the bright seeds of the board schools – so called because they were administered by local boards of elected governors – had the wholly beneficial effect that Holmes predicted for them. Such seeds may grow into minds equipped with only a little learning but ready to question all established values whether they have anything better to offer or not. If the board schools were lighthouses, they were also deep-sapping mine shafts. And towers before long were to tilt and tumble.

That same year of 1870 saw, too, another development much appreciated by Sherlock Holmes once his work had begun in earnest. This was the nation-wide establishment of the telegraph system, enabling him to flash inquiries and directions from one end of the country to the other. But the blessing, again, was double-edged. It was one more contribution to an ever-speeding rate of life. 'Telegrams and anger', the novelist E. M. Forster was to exclaim in dismay just forty years later.

The increasing number of cheap newspapers was yet another symptom of the same soon-to-be-dizzying rush. Readers were increasingly eager. The Tichborne scandal of 1871, that extraordinary claim to a great estate by the impostor Arthur Orton, former cattle-slaughterer of Wagga Wagga, Australia,

seized on the public imagination right through until 1874 as no other legal action had done since the impeachment of Warren Hastings ninety years earlier. But, in the years that followed, other law-court revelations (when, Watson would tell us, events had escaped the behind-the-scenes attentions of Mr Sherlock Holmes) were to be almost as greedily devoured.

Charles Darwin.

The years around 1870 saw, too, the disappearance of many giant pillars of the time before. In 1870 itself Dickens died, that marvellous chronicler among other things of the Victorian home at its Christmasiest. Tennyson and Browning lived for twenty years more, but in both the high creative flare was reduced after 1870 to flickering point. So, too, was the fire that had burned up, in tortuous flames, in Carlyle.

The Tichborne Claimant arrives for one of the sittings of the trial that seized the imagination of a public beginning to be avid for scandals.

A final major work that appeared just one year after 1870 was Charles Darwin's *Descent of Man*, the book that extended to

human beings his theory of natural selection, propounded, to revolutionary effect, in *The Origin of Species* in 1859. It was this scientific challenge to the simple world-picture of the Old Testament, seen by a large majority till then as an article of faith, that was to do more, probably, than any other single work to make the apparently secure world of the mid-century run with fissures. It was a work that lay beneath the outward manifestation of Sherlock Holmes as much as the Bible lay beneath the personality of, let us say, John Bunyan.

For Holmes was, to the bone, a man of his time. As such he lived, too, in convinced opposition to that huge sliding-away through which he was to pursue his career. He was a knight-champion called forth by the hour to combat the dragon that, about that year 1870, broke through the bars that had seemed so securely to constrain it. It is the story of his single-handed combat, mighty yet doomed, that we have to tell.

Holmes's first case, the *Gloria Scott* affair, was a premonitory instance. It began by the oddest of coincidences. And perhaps, had it not happened the way it did, Watson tells us, Holmes would never have actually embarked on the career for which he had been preparing himself, 'moping in my rooms and working out my own little methods of thought'.

One morning as the young recluse went down to chapel – inescapable duty for any undergraduate in those religion-permeated days – Victor Trevor's bull-terrier froze on to his ankle. Penitent Trevor went often in the following ten days, while Holmes was 'laid by the heels', to inquire, and a mild friendship developed culminating in an invitation to Trevor's father's place in Norfolk. During that visit Holmes, challenged by old Mr Trevor, demonstrated a little of the methods he had taught himself. He claimed first that his friend's father was going about in fear of some personal attack, second that he had boxed a good deal in his youth, third that he had done a considerable amount of digging at some time, and lastly that he had been acquainted once with someone whose initials were J. A. whom he had been desperately anxious to forget.

Old Mr Trevor was, of course, astonished to find this young man knew so much about him, and about his secrets. Holmes explained he had done no more than exercise the habits of observation and inference he had been endeavouring to inculcate in himself, with, be it noted, that tireless application characteristic of the best in his age. The fear of attack he had deduced from the newish stick which the old man invariably

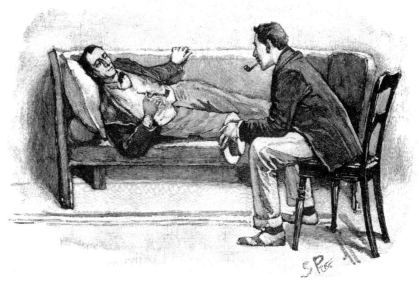

carried, within its head a hole bored to take melted lead. The boxing was deduced from 'the peculiar flattening and thickening' of the subject's ears, the digging from the callosities on his hands. And the acquaintanceship with one 'J.A.' had come from a swift glimpse of a partially blotted-out tattoo in the bend of the old man's elbow.

'I don't know how you manage this, Mr Holmes,' old Trevor said, 'but it seems to me that all the detectives of fact and fancy would be children in your hands.' And at that moment the young man's vague aspirations crystallized.

Some seven weeks after this vacation visit, weeks Holmes had spent in rooms in London experimenting in organic chemistry, a telegram came from young Trevor imploring him to return with all urgency. Back in Norfolk his college friend, now thin and careworn, greeted him with the words 'The governor is dying.' Old Trevor's state had been brought about, it seemed, by the presence in the house of a man who had called there on the evening before Holmes's departure and who shortly afterwards had been installed as butler.

'Do you know who it was we let into the house that day?' young Trevor asked.

'I have no idea.'

'It was the Devil, Holmes!'

Already we see, evil had begun to prowl through one cosy, safe Victorian home. And at once the man who was to devote himself for long years ahead to combating what he was often to call 'devilry' threw himself into the struggle.

Young Trevor inquires after the undergraduate Holmes, whose ankle was bitten by Trevor's bull-terrier. A Paget illustration to the *Gloria Scott* account.

The key to the
Gloria Scott riddle
in Holmes's hands.

As it turned out, he did not have to use his methods to any great extent in order to solve the mystery. Arriving at the house, the two young men found old Trevor dead with beside him a letter he had received that morning which had apparently precipitated his end. The letter seemed to young Trevor, and to Holmes at first, a mere unintelligible farrago. But Holmes did not need to apply his logic to it for long before, in an instant, he had the key to the riddle in his hands. It was in fact a coded message telling the old man, whose past proved from papers he had left to have been shadowed by an episode of mutiny aboard the convict barque *Gloria Scott*, to fly.

Holmes's powers had hardly been called upon. But he had been given a chance to test them on a real mystery and had confirmed his ambition of setting up as a scientific detective. He was to be a figure in considerable contrast to the persistent but seldom very intelligent police detectives of the day, and in yet more contrast to the rabble of private inquiry agents of the time, great snoopers on cheating mistresses, trudging hunters of missing daughters.

Because it was science, applied science, that very Victorian characteristic, that was to be the young consulting detective's most bruited weapon in the struggle he had committed himself to. He was to be yet one more participant in a whole stream of technological inventions of a useful nature. There was the typewriter in 1867. The telephone in 1876. In 1877 the gramophone. In 1879 the electric light bulb, invented by Swan in England simultaneously with Edison in America. In Germany at this time Benz and Daimler were working towards the internal-combustion engine which was to begin its society-shaking career in the 1880s. In the years between 1870 and 1888 the bicycle was brought to perfection. From 1860 or so Sir Henry Bessemer's revolutionary steel-making process led to the possibility of building huge structures like the Forth Bridge. In 1856 the eighteen-year-old W. H. Perkin had discovered the first aniline dye, a derivative of coal-tar, and a revolution began that put Victorian ladies, and Edwardian ladies after them, into dozens of new hectic shades of purple, green and blue. Even the great theoretical scientist, Lord Kelvin, in 1866 plain William Thomson, received his knighthood for his work on the transatlantic cable. And, according to Dr Watson, in 1881 Holmes himself was to discover a reagent precipitated only by haemoglobin, thus producing a certain means of detecting even the tiniest quantity of blood.

But that is a little to jump ahead in our account of his career. Established in London, in rooms in Montague Street hard by the British Museum, Holmes found at first little work though he wrote occasionally. There was an article for a magazine about his methods of observation and analysis called 'The Book of Life'

New Year greetings by the new-fangled telephone.

21

and a monograph – the first of not a few – *Upon the Distinction Between the Ashes of the Various Tobaccos: An Enumeration of 140 Forms of Cigar, Cigarette and Pipe Tobacco, with Coloured Plates illustrating the Differences in the Ash.*

Only rarely did a case interrupt his studies 'in all those branches of science which might make me more efficient'. In 1879 there was the affair of the Musgrave Ritual, another business where a university acquaintance led to employment, though hardly one calling on his most characteristic powers for all that it resulted in the rediscovery of the ancient crown of the Kings of England. There were, too, the Tarleton Murders, the case of Vamberry, the wine-merchant, as well as the business of Ricoletti of the club-foot and his abominable wife and the adventure of the old Russian woman, about none of which we know more than Watson's bare mention years later of their names. And of the singular affair of the aluminium crutch it need be noted only that it took place before the discovery, by C.M. Hall in America in 1886 and simultaneously by Héroult in France, of an economic method of separating this lightest of metals from its ore.

But in 1881 there did occur an event in Holmes's life of no enormous significance in itself but of cardinal importance to all those of us who have later delighted in his exploits. In that year, perhaps on New Year's Day itself, he was introduced to his future biographer, Dr John H. Watson.

Watson at the time of the inspired meeting was an Army medical officer recovering in London from the effects of enteric fever, 'that curse of our Indian possessions', and from a wound received at the Battle of Maiwand in 1880, one of the few defeats British forces suffered in the intermittent conflicts in Afghanistan aimed at checking the spread of Russian power towards India, over which only four years before Queen Victoria had with much pomp been proclaimed Empress.

At Maiwand a force of 2,400 troops had been attacked by Afghans outnumbering them by ten to one and had lost some 1,100 men. The Afghans had gone on to besiege Kandahar. But General Sir Frederick Roberts, a v.c. of the Indian Mutiny days, had then marched 10,000 men 313 miles in twenty-two days, totally to rout the besiegers.

Roberts, 'Bobs' to his men and soon to his idolaters all over the Empire, became one of that pantheon held up to glorify the rapidly expanding Imperial dream. Six years later he was to march another British army against a native enemy, this time down the road to Mandalay with the annexation of Burmah to

Above: General Roberts, 'Bobs' to his men, with his officers during the Second Afghan War of 1878–80.

Left: At bay in Afghanistan. An *Illustrated London News* artist's impression.

crown the adventure. Later still, in 1900, as Lord Roberts of Kandahar, he was to retrieve a different adverse situation for his countrymen, this time in South Africa, when in a series of victories he defeated the forces of the Boers and relieved the encircled town of Mafeking. There was then such jubilation in distant London, shocked in its pride that any foreign force could black true Britons' eyes, that it was proposed even in advance of

Mafeking Night in London.

final victory to grant Roberts the immense sum of £100,000 and the hysteria in the streets brought into existence a new verb, 'to maffick', a word that stayed in the language for many a year to come.

On a pension of eleven shillings and sixpence a day, Dr Watson was finding a London hotel too expensive, and, bemoaning his situation to a chance-met acquaintance, one

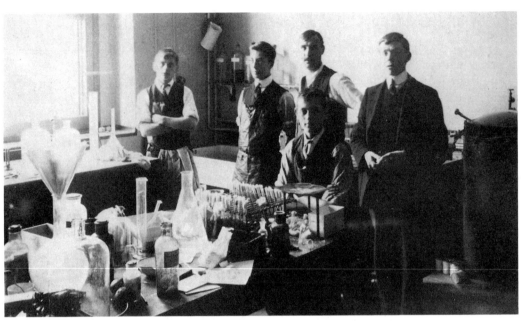

Laboratory at St Bartholomew's Hospital ('Bart's') at about the time Holmes and Watson first met.

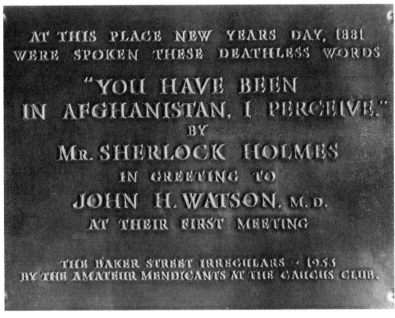

AT THIS PLACE NEW YEARS DAY, 1881
WERE SPOKEN THESE DEATHLESS WORDS

"YOU HAVE BEEN
IN AFGHANISTAN, I PERCEIVE."
BY
Mr. SHERLOCK HOLMES
IN GREETING TO
JOHN H. WATSON. M.D.
AT THEIR FIRST MEETING

THE BAKER STREET IRREGULARS ~ 1953
BY THE AMATEUR MENDICANTS AT THE CAUCUS CLUB.

The plaque at Bart's, commemorating the first meeting of Holmes and
Dr Watson

Stamford who had been a dresser under him at Bart's, the equivalent of a houseman, or intern, in today's hospitals, he learnt of a strange young researcher looking for someone to share rooms with in Baker Street. Stamford took his friend to Bart's and there in the chemical laboratory the first encounter between Holmes and Watson took place, at a spot marked today not unfittingly by a substantial metal plaque.

It was an enormous piece of luck for all those of us who have come to admire, or even idolize, Sherlock Holmes that the person who joined him in those 'couple of comfortable bedrooms with a single large airy sitting-room, cheerfully furnished and illuminated by two broad windows' was the man he was. He was every bit as tolerant as he needed to be. And that was considerably. By the time they were well established Watson found that Holmes was 'in his personal habits one of the most untidy men that ever drove a fellow-lodger to distraction' with cigars in the coal-scuttle, tobacco in the toe of a Persian slipper, unanswered correspondence transfixed with a jack-knife to the mantelpiece and eventually the significantly patriotic letters VR bullet-pocked on a wall as pistol practice.

The sitting-room at 221B Baker Street, as reconstructed for a Festival of Britain exhibition in 1951.

Then Watson's ordinariness – again and again he shows himself to be the very pattern of normality – and his calm acted as an ideal foil to a temperament almost exactly the opposite. An intelligence no more than average made Holmes's brilliant brain take fire like steel touched to grindstone. And finally Watson was the very embodiment of all those values that Holmes, it is not too much to say, existed to defend – honesty, straightforwardness, justice ('Watson, you are a British jury,' Holmes cried at the climax of one of their adventures), courage, courtesy, sobriety, decency. He was to the core an English gentleman.

But there is one small flaw in what might seem to us a perfect conjunction. When Watson came to chronicle the adventures of his friend he proved quite frequently to be startlingly inaccurate, far beyond the distortion that writing of past days often brings. His narrations are generally much better than we would have any right to expect from a simple general practitioner. Each story is unfolded by telling us what we need to know just when we need to know it. The style is a good straightforward English that rises every now and again imperceptibly to a quiet phrase of extraordinary effectiveness. But there are mistakes. On one occasion (while relating the adventure 'A Scandal in Bohemia') Watson calls Mrs Hudson, the landlady of the Baker Street rooms who served Holmes with exemplary faithfulness for all the twenty-odd years of his tenancy, Mrs Turner. On another occasion (during the adventure of *The Sign of Four*) he tells us within six pages that it is both July and September. Once he begins two accounts, those of 'The Resident Patient' and 'The Cardboard Box', with exactly the same opening paragraphs. Yet errors such as these are a small price to pay for the wealth that his chronicles eventually provided for us.

What they brought us first, even before the initial adventure the two of them were to share had got under way, was a list Watson drew up of his curious fellow lodger's qualities. It is worth looking at in some detail.

Its first three items state that Holmes's knowledge of literature, philosophy and astronomy was 'Nil', even down to complete ignorance of the solar system. But here we must suspect that the sparklingly quick detective was teasing his companion – it was not to be the last time he did so – and that, although he preferred to keep to the fore subjects more pertinent to his unique profession, he was as well up in general information as any man of his age. Or better. Before Watson has recounted many more of his exploits we will have heard him quote in the original the German of Goethe (much better known in pre-1914 England

Opposite: E.W. Barton-Wright (left) demonstrating the Japanese self-defence system he named bartisu. From an article in *Pearson's Magazine*, 1899.

than he is now, but still not exactly man-in-the-street stuff) and the French of Flaubert as well as refer learnedly to the works of Carlyle, after, when Watson had quoted him earlier, he had 'inquired in the naïvest way who he might be and what he had done'.

But 'Knowledge of Politics – Feeble' we can more or less accept, though Holmes later was to have dealings with statesmen and potentates not a few and to show no signs of groping. Of the sciences of botany, geology, chemistry and anatomy we will not be surprised to find his knowledge profound, if variable and essentially on the applied side. Nor will it be unexpected that he has 'a good practical knowledge of British law'. Two other attributes, however, would seem to be somewhat in opposition. Holmes, Watson tells us, was an expert with the singlestick, that yard-long basket-hilted staff used for training in sabre-fighting, as well as a boxer and a swordsman (and in the 1880s the sword had by no means disappeared as a weapon) and we learn later that he was, too, an exponent of 'baritsu, or the Japanese system of wrestling' (though the author of a contemporary magazine article on Japanese methods of self-defence, one E. W. Barton-Wright, gave the system a Japanese-English name based on his own, bartisu). But, Watson adds, his new friend also 'plays the violin well'.

The sword and the violin. Holmes, as we shall see, was very much a man of two sides. Indeed, Watson had already noted that 'nothing could exceed his energy when the working fit was on him', bouts he would later call 'outflames of nervous energy which could make him on occasion both the most active and the strongest man that I have ever known', but that at times, too, 'for days on end he would lie upon the sofa'.

Finally, Watson's list tells us that Holmes's knowledge of sensational literature was 'immense'. Sensational literature comprised those myriad accounts of crimes of all sorts which had poured from the presses ever since printing had become cheap. They were accounts produced in response to the longing, shared by almost all of us, to learn about those of our fellows with hardihood enough to break the rules which living in a society necessarily imposes. And this longing, curiously, lies at the root of the success of crime fiction, which Watson's accounts of Holmes's activities were largely responsible for making respectable reading.

The vogue for their less respectable forerunners can be traced to the Reverend John Vilette, Chaplain at Newgate Prison, who in 1776 wrote four volumes of *The Annals of Newgate, or, the*

THE

CHRONICLES OF NEWGATE

BY

ARTHUR GRIFFITHS

MAJOR LATE 63RD REGIMENT; ONE OF H.M. INSPECTORS OF PRISONS
AUTHOR OF "THE MEMORIALS OF MILLBANK," ETC., ETC.

IN TWO VOLUMES.—VOL. I.

LONDON: CHAPMAN AND HALL
(LIMITED)
1884

Malefactors' Register, accounts of murderers, thieves and others to whom he had ministered in gaol. Soon his choicest crimes were being produced as broadsheets to sell at a penny apiece and others, both true or fairly true and grossly invented, were swiftly added. The best-known of the purveyors of such accounts was James Catnach, whose *Last Dying Speech of William Corder* (the Red Barn murderer) is said to have sold more than a million copies in 1828. And, of course, as printing became even cheaper newspapers began to reach downwards through the layers of society, publishing, as they did so, more and more accounts of crimes likely to appeal to a wide readership. Before long there were papers like the *Illustrated Police News*, solely devoted to the topic. But even at the journalistic heights the subject was not despised. Delane, Editor of *The Times* from 1841 to 1877, once wrote to his deputy when he had been away, 'you have been lucky in having so many murders.'

Holmes's immense knowledge of such apparently trivial writings shows him as seeking not only the *modus operandi* but also the human motive in every sort of crime, analysing and classifying. Frequently, Watson tells us, faced with a current mystery he refers to some old, almost forgotten parallel case and gets a clue to the solution. He was the first of the criminal sociologists.

Let us follow him now as he embarks, with the trusty Watson, on the first case they pursued together, the affair which Watson later, seizing on a phrase of his friend's, was to entitle *A Study in Scarlet*. It shows us a good deal of what was characteristic in the methods of the consulting detective and of his world.

The matter began with the delivery of a note at No. 221B Baker Street from Inspector Gregson, 'the smartest of the Scotland Yarders' as Holmes called him. It is said there has been 'a bad business during the night . . . off the Brixton Road.' The body of a well-dressed man had been found without any apparent wound on him although the bare walls all round were spattered with blood. Holmes is trapped in one of his moods of lethargy, but Watson at length succeeds in stirring him to action and the two of them set off for the scene in a hansom, that speedy two-wheeled two-passenger horse-cab with the driver seated high up behind that was to be Holmes's most usual form of transport in the thousands of close-packed London streets. Now they drive through a day in which, in one of Watson's occasional glowing phrases, 'a dun-coloured veil hung over the house-tops, looking like the reflection of the mud-coloured streets beneath.'

To Watson's surprise, Holmes halts the cab at some distance

Opposite: Sensational literature. The frontispiece of an 1884 volume.

from the house and instead of hurrying in he 'lounged up and down the pavement, and gazed vacantly at the ground'. But, once inside, he acts with gratifying vigour, examining the corpse with fingers 'flying here, there and everywhere, feeling, pressing, unbuttoning', stooping even to sniff at the dead man. Soon, however, Gregson's rival, little, lean, ferret-like Inspector Lestrade, claims he has made a discovery that will swiftly end the mystery. He shows them, scrawled in blood in a dark corner, the letters RACHE. They stand for 'Rachel', he says. It will be just a question of *cherchez la femme*. Unperturbed, Holmes continues with his minute inspection of the room, pausing only when as the body is lifted to be carried away a gold ring is discovered.

When he has finished he turns to the two Scotland Yarders and says: 'There has been murder done, and the murderer was a man. He was more than six feet high, was in the prime of life, had small feet for his height, wore coarse, square-toed boots and smoked a Trichinopoly cigar. He came here with his victim in a

Opposite: The Strand about 1898. Note the telegraph office Holmes would often have used.

A hansom and a four-wheeled 'growler', London cabs of the 1880s.

four-wheeled cab, which was drawn by a horse with three old
shoes and a new one on his off fore-leg. In all probability the
murderer had a florid face, and the finger nails of his right hand
were remarkably long.' He adds that the murder was committed
by poison. And 'One other thing, Lestrade. "Rache" is the
German for "revenge".'

But Holmes, it quickly proves, is teasing Lestrade here, much
as he has teased Watson. After dispatching from the nearest
telegraph office a long telegram, about which he tells his
companion nothing, he hurries off by cab to question the
constable who first discovered the body. On the way he points
out that although the bloody scrawl was written in capitals
resembling the German black-letter, in fact 'a real German
invariably prints in the Latin character, so that we may safely
say that this was not written by one, but by a clumsy imitator
who overdid his part.' Observation, not of superficial
appearances but of the real facts, triumphs.

The conversation had taken place while the cab 'had been
threading its way through a long succession of dingy streets and
dreary byways. In the dingiest and dreariest of them our driver
suddenly came to a stand. "That's Audley Court in there," he
said, pointing to a narrow slit in the line of dead-coloured brick.'

The constable on the beat in the 1880s, if not quite as low in
the social scale as the unskilled labourers who made up one in
three of the first regular London police force, the peelers,
founded by Sir Robert Peel in 1829, was still a pretty humble and

35

BULL'S EYE ON BOBBY.

Mr. Bull (takes Policeman's lantern). "THANK YOU. I'LL JUST HAVE A LOOK ROUND MYSELF. STRIKES ME THE PREMISES AIN'T AS CLEAN AS THEY MIGHT BE!"

Punch comment on corruption at Scotland Yard in the late 1870s.

poorly paid fellow. Gilbert's song from *The Pirates of Penzance*, written in 1880, a year earlier than the date of this first Watson adventure, had a good deal of truth in it: a policeman's lot was not a happy one. A constable's maximum pay was only 23*s*. 4*d*. a week (compare it with Watson's modest 11*s*. 6*d*. a day) and for this he was on duty seven days a week. It was not until 1910 that Parliament passed the Police Forces (Weekly Rest-day) Act. So it is perhaps little wonder that there had been a police strike, short-lived and sharply punished, in London in 1872. But the man on the beat was kept at it by the prospect of a small pension, rare at that level of society then, and he was, too, often able to augment his income with tips. 'Walter', that veracious chronicler of sexual adventure of the period, more than once speaks of giving 'Mr Policeman' a shilling to turn a blind eye.

Gregson and Lestrade would have been paid only some four times a constable's wage, and it is scarcely surprising that in 1878 three out of four chief inspectors of the Detective Branch, as it was then called, had been found guilty of corruption. In the aftermath of their trial a separate Criminal Investigation Department had been formed, working until 1891 from a building off Whitehall Place in Scotland Yard (once the lodgings allocated to visiting Scottish monarchs) and after that from New Scotland Yard, the building designed by the fashionable Norman Shaw on the Victoria Embankment on the site of a proposed but never completed opera-house.

But even the new C.I.D.'s reputation was not high. *Punch*

delighted to refer to it as the Defective Department, and it had to combat, too, a strong prejudice against having any detectives at all. In 1869 the then Commissioner of Metropolitan Police had commented that a detective system would be 'viewed with the greatest suspicion by the majority of Englishmen and is, in fact, entirely foreign to the habits and feelings of the nation.'

So neither Holmes nor Watson can have been surprised that in order to visit Police Constable John Rance they had to negotiate

Great Scotland Yard in 1895, the building occupied by the Metropolitan Police Criminal Investigation Department until 1891.

New Scotland Yard, the headquarters for the Metropolitan Police built by Norman Shaw and occupied until 1967.

a courtyard lined by sordid dwellings, skirt round groups of dirty children and duck past discoloured washing. From Rance, with the aid of a half-sovereign which Holmes had taken from his pocket and pensively played with, they learnt that 'an uncommon drunk sort o' man' had been propped up outside the murder house shortly after the discovery of the body, though the constable had not thought to mention this to his superiors.

'The man whom you held in your hands is the man who holds the clue of this mystery,' Holmes tells the unlucky Rance. 'There is no use of arguing about it now; I tell you that it is so.'

And then, awaiting the answer to his mysterious telegram, he spends the afternoon at the St James's Hall lost in listening to Madame Norman-Neruda, perhaps the greatest violinist of her day, later to marry her conductor on this occasion and as Mme Hallé to be appointed Violinist to the Queen. 'It was magnificent,' he says of the concert as he and Watson sit down to dinner. 'Do you remember what Darwin says about music? He claims that the power of producing and appreciating it existed among the human race long before the power of speech was arrived at.'

Holmes lost in listening to music.

Alfred Tennyson: the
Julia Margaret Cameron
photograph.

T.H. Huxley, from the *Vanity Fair*
cartoon series 'Men of the Day'.

Mme Norman-Neruda.

This thought of Darwin's, so striking to Holmes if we are to trust Watson's later account, is to be found in that last major work of his, *The Descent of Man*, the book which reinforced the tremendous effect of his earlier thesis that progress came through 'the survival of the fittest' and that man was descended not only from the apes but even from primordial slime. 'The consciousness of this great truth weighs like a nightmare', wrote Darwin's disciple, T.H. Huxley, 'upon many of the best minds of these days. They watch what they conceive to be the progress of materialism, in such fear and powerless anger as the savage feels, when, during an eclipse, the great shadow creeps over the face of the sun.' Tennyson, that 'best mind' and ever wind-answering harp of his time, lamented in his *Maud*:

> *For nature is one with rapine, a harm no preacher can heal;*
> *The Mayfly is torn by the swallow, the sparrow spear'd by the shrike,*
> *And the whole little wood where I sit is a world of plunder and prey.*
> *We are puppets, Man in his pride, and Beauty fair in her flower;*
> *Do we move ourselves, or are moved by an unseen hand at a game*
> *That pushes us off from the board, and others ever succeed?*

And where the best minds went, lesser minds soon followed. Darwin's teachings rapidly became the jargon of the day, undermining everywhere. A.J. Balfour, one day to be Prime Minister, noted as a young man that even his barber rattled on about 'evolution, Darwin and Huxley and the lot of them – hashed up somehow with the good time coming and the universal brotherhood.' That vague feeling that the long-fixed order of things was soon to tumble and Jack become as good as his master was to produce concrete manifestations with which Holmes, champion of order, Darwinian though he was, found himself locked in combat on many, many occasions in the years to come. In a Darwinian world the beasts could be kept from roaming where they would only by the ceaseless exercise of reason coupled with that indefinable but powerful quality, decency. They were Holmes's weapons.

But on that night of 4 March 1881 Holmes was not left for long to muse over the dinner-table on primitive man, music-lover and child of the apes. In answer to advertisements he had inserted in every evening newspaper – how smoothly the world worked in those days, and what splendid use Holmes was to make, both in advertising and in finding the hidden in advertisements, of what he called 'the apocrypha of the agony column' – a visitor arrived to claim the gold ring that had been found under the corpse in the house off the Brixton Road. But here Holmes experiences a

LG.—Mizpah has heard nothing since October and is in great distress. Send letter and topaz care O. 28 mills.

GARROD'S FRIEND.—If you go to America this year don't entirely forget me.

IF this should MEET the EYE of GEORGE WILLIAMS, he is requested to SEND his ADDRESS to Mr. Clark, No. 131, Euston-road, London, N.W., where a letter awaits him of great importance.

CHARLES HUMPAGE, deceased.—The CHILDREN of CHARLES HUMPAGE, late of Moor-green Mills, in the county of Worcester, Metal Roller, who died on the 19th June, 1854, and the issue of such of them as have since died, are requested to COMMUNICATE forthwith with me, the undersigned, when they will hear of something to their advantage. Dated this 1st day of July, 1881.—MATTHEW JOHN BLEWITT, Solicitor, 5, Waterloo-street, Birmingham.

A TELEGRAM for JOHN HANNAH KILLEAD, Antrim, from Robert, Melbourne, has been received by Reuter's Telegram Company (Limited), 24, Old Jewry, London, but CANNOT be DELIVERED through insufficient address.

THREE to ONE ; left, right ; red through green to black.—A gentleman, investigating the relation of Freemasonry to liberty and progress, will be glad to communicate with others studying the same subject. Address C. H. Lake, Queenslea, Liverpool-road, Kingston-hill, Surrey.

BANK of ENGLAND.—Unclaimed Dividend.—Application having been made to the Governors of the Bank of England to direct the payment of one dividend on the sum of £5,600 Consolidated £3 per Cent. Annuities, heretofore standing in the name of ALBERT SMITH, of Camden-house, Chatham, Gentleman, and which dividend was paid over to the Commissioners for the Reduction of the National Debt in consequence of having remained unclaimed since the 5th January, 1871 ;—Notice is hereby given that, on the expiration of three months from this date (July 4, 1881), the said Dividend will be Paid to Albert Smith, who has claimed the same, unless some other claimant shall sooner appear and make out his claim thereto.

ROYAL GENERAL THEATRICAL FUND.—The Directors gratefully ACKNOWLEDGE the RECEIPT, through Henry Irving, Esq., of ONE HUNDRED POUNDS from Admiral the Hon. Carr Glyn, C.B., C.S.I., in remembrance of the late Miss Neilson.

NORTH-EASTERN HOSPITAL for CHILDREN, Hackney-road, E.—The Committee gratefully ACKNOWLEDGE a DONATION of FIVE GUINEAS from Messrs. G. Cawston and Co.—ALFRED NIXON, Secretary.

ROYAL HOSPITAL for DISEASES of the CHEST, City-road.—The Treasurer and Council thankfully ACKNOWLEDGE the RECEIPT of an anonymous DONATION of FIVE POUNDS, per the Treasurer, and of a new Annual Subscription of Three Guineas from Geo. P. Bidder, Esq.

PROPOSED SCARLET FEVER CONVALESCENT HOME.—The Committee gratefully ACKNOWLEDGE the RECEIPT of ONE HUNDRED POUNDS from the Right Hon. W. E. and Mrs. Gladstone.—MARY WARDELL, Hon. Sec.—2, Stanley-gardens, Belsize, N.W.

THE VICTORIA HOSPITAL for CHILDREN, Queen's-road, Chelsea, and Churchfields, Margate.—Patroness —H.R.H. the PRINCESS LOUISE.—A further DONATION of TEN POUNDS, from Thos. Rippingall, Esq., is gratefully ACKNOWLEDGED by the Committee of Management.—COMMANDER BLOUNT, R.N., Secretary.

LOST, 23d ult., at St. George's-hall, a RUBY-COLOURED SCENT BOTTLE. Whoever returns it to 31, Redcliffe-gardens, shall be REWARDED.

TEN POUNDS REWARD.—LOST, on 30th June, at Henley-on-Thames Railway Station, a GOLD LEVER HUNTER ; Maker, John Carter, Cornhill, No. 4442, with inscription on medallion outside, " Presented by Frederick Probst to his friend Wm. Man." Whoever will take the same to Mr. John Carter, 61, Cornhill, shall receive the above reward.

FOUND, in Porchester-road, Bayswater, a PURSE, containing a bank-note, gold, &c., and a small piece of paper with a number on it. Apply to Messrs. Chandler, Pixley, and Co., No. 15, Coleman-street, E.C.

FOUND, near Victoria Station, on Friday afternoon, a PURSE, containing money, &c. The owner can have it by giving description and paying cost of this advertisement.—Mr. Emmens, 49, Ebury-street.

A GRAND EXHIBITION and SALE of ART-NEEDLEWORK, Paintings on China, Satin, &c., will be held, under distinguished patronage, at the Town-hall, High-street, Kensington, on Tuesday and Wednesday, July 5th and 6th. Open at 10 a.m. Admission, on Tuesday, 2s. 6d.; after 6 p.m. 1s.; on Wednesday, 2s., after 6 p.m. 6d.

DECORATIVE ART EXHIBITION, at the New Galleries, 103, New Bond-street, comprising Oil Pictures and water-

said William Williams.)

The persons claiming to be entitled to the said remaining debts are, by their solicitors, on or before the 26th day of April, 1881, to come in and prove their claims at the Chambers of the Vice Chancellor Sir Richard Malins, situate at No. 12, Staple-inn, Middlesex, or in default thereof they will be peremptorily excluded from the benefit of the said Order. Monday, the 9th day of May, 1881, at Three o'clock, at the said Chambers, is appointed for hearing and adjudicating upon the claims.—Dated this 28th day of February, 1881.

EDWARD SHEARME, Chief Clerk.

LEACH and DEEDES, 10, Lancaster-place, Strand, London, Solicitors for persons having the conduct of the proceedings.

NOTICE.— Considering the frequency wherewith objets d'art and literary works have, without permission, been forwarded to His Majesty the Emperor of Austria-Hungary, as well as to other members of the Imperial and Royal Family, the undersigned desires to draw attention to the following rule which should be observed by persons residing in the British Empire, who intend to submit any article to the Imperial and Royal Court :—In every case application must first be made to the Chief Chamberlain, through the Austro-Hungarian Embassy in London, for permission to forward anything whatever. The exact nature of the objects sought to be forwarded should be fully specified, and no such article should be despatched until the receipt of a reply announcing that the desired permission has been granted. No notice can be taken of any articles which have been or may be forwarded contrary to the foregoing directions.—29, St. Swithin's-lane, E.C. The Imperial and Royal Austro-Hungarian Deputy-Consul-General, F. KRAFF.

DUNBAR v. DUNBAR.—With reference to the advertisement published on the 1st instant, in which Archdeacon Dunbar alleges this suit was the result of a wicked conspiracy, Mrs. Dunbar, in reply, asserts the statement to be false, and will be so proved in the event of Archdeacon Dunbar venturing to justify his statement by legal proceedings. The special jury who tried the case, while stating they were constrained, in consequence of insufficient evidence, to find for the respondent, expressed personally to Mrs. Dunbar their extreme sympathy with her.—LEWIS and LEWIS, 10 and 11, Ely-place, Holborn, Solicitors for Mrs. Dunbar.

HALL-MARKING.—The attention of Members of Parliament is requested to the following :—" Until lately the wisdom and perfectness of the Hall-mark were not called in question, but now a very serious case is made out against it, as being both clumsy and inefficient, and as operating in restraint of trade. It is evaded, forged, transferred, hard to understand, easy to imitate ; is extended to very base alloys, and in various ways so used as to deceive the unwary. In other words, it is not the safeguard it pretends to be."—(Evening Standard, Feb. 28.)

EDWARD J. WATHERSTON, 12, Pall-mall-east, London.

MOORS, Forests, and Fishings.—E. PATON and SON, Gun and Rifle Makers and Agents for Shootings, beg to announce their LIST of SPORTING QUARTERS to be LET, for 1881, which is forwarded, post free, on application. Proprietors having shootings to let are respectfully solicited for particulars. Address No. 108. Mount-street, Grosvenor-square, London, W. ; 44, George-street, Perth ; and 37, Church-street, Inverness. N.B.—This is the largest shooting agency in the United Kingdom.

NEXT of KIN.—£70,000,000 Unclaimed.—A REGISTER, containing the names of all persons advertised for to claim money and property since 1700, post free 2s. 1d.—DOUGAL and Co., 28, Francis-street, W.C. Wills searched.

NEXT of KIN.—1881 Edition.—£77,000,000 Unclaimed.—A REGISTER containing the names of 41,000 persons who have been advertised for to claim property and money since 1700. Post free 2s. 1d.—DOUGAL and Co., 223, Strand, W.C.

PRIVATE INQUIRY OFFICE (high-class and old-established).—Mr. WARD, Chandos-chambers, 22, Buckingham-street, Strand, London.

LLOYD'S MISSING FRIENDS' INQUIRY and GENERAL AGENCY OFFICE, Melbourne, Victoria, Australia.

THE FUNERAL of the late M. R. MEYER, Esq., of 4, Highbury-hill, and 16, Mark-lane, will take place at Highgate Cemetery, on Saturday next, the 5th inst., at half-past 12 o'clock.

FUNERALS.—Messrs. T. H. FILMER and SON, 31 and 32, Berners-street, W., beg to say they conduct FUNERALS either in town or country. Established 1820.

FUNERALS.—Messrs. BECKETT and SON'S superior system of funerals, with elegance, refinement, and economy. The most recherché funeral furnishers extant guaranteed.—Warehouse, corner of the Prince of Wales and Kentish-town roads, N.W.

REFORMED FUNERALS.—The FUNERAL COMPANY was established in 1843 for funeral economy and reform. Offices, 28, New Bridge-street, E.C., and 82, Baker-street, W. ALEXIS BONO, General Manager.

THE SIMPLIFICATION of FUNERALS and the PROPER BURIAL of the DEAD.—Explanatory pamphlet gratis on application.—LONDON NECROPOLIS COMPANY, 2, Lancaster-place, Strand, W.C. Patent Earth to Earth coffins.

Agony columns from *The Times*.

check. The visitor turns out to be, not the tall florid-faced murderer he had been expecting, but a very old and wrinkled woman. Or so she seems. Because when Holmes and Watson set out to follow her she skilfully evades them. 'We were old women to be so taken in,' Holmes exclaims ruefully. 'It must have been a young man, and an active one, too, besides being an incomparable actor. The get-up was inimitable.' Nor will this be the last time the great detective is temporarily tricked. If he was in some sort a superman, he was also always human.

But in principle Holmes is soon proved perfectly right about the case, though not before another death occurs, again with the word 'Rache' written 'in letters of blood'. Holmes needed here, too, to make use of other talents than his own. On the second day of the affair as he was breakfasting with Watson there came the sound of many pattering steps on the stairs, accompanied by 'audible expressions of disgust' from Mrs Hudson, and there entered, in Watson's words, 'half a dozen of the dirtiest and most ragged street arabs that ever I clapped eyes on.' They are what Holmes calls 'the Baker Street Irregulars', his eyes and ears all over teeming London.

The street arab. He is perhaps the very bottom of the great pyramid of late Victorian society which Holmes's adventures took him up and down, down and up, from a visit to a certain gracious lady at Windsor to his meetings with these small-fry scum and to his long walks 'which appeared to take him into the lowest portions of the city', walks which gave him his unrivalled

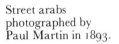

Street arabs photographed by Paul Martin in 1893.

An East End opium
den. Gustave Doré's
etching of 1872.

knowledge of the by-ways of huge, sprawling, murky London
and gave him, too, perhaps, a curious pleasure shared with,
among a good many others of that day, Gustave Doré, the great
French illustrator, and Charles Dickens.

Up the pyramid and down. Holmes in his time was to
encounter both the most degraded, like the woman he brought to
the light of day during the adventure of the Illustrious Client
who said 'I'm easy to find. "Hell, London" gets me every time',
to the highest, the owners of vast estates and the wielders of the
greatest political power. And he was to encounter oddities, too.
A tide-waiter, on watch till a ship that needed rummaging for
smuggled goods came to dock. A journalist and duellist who

A cab yard such as the one where Jefferson Hope hired himself out as a driver in order to track down his victims.

ended stark mad looking down at a matchbox containing 'a remarkable worm, said to be unknown to science'. A retired colourman. A gasfitter. A danseuse at the Allegro. A penny-a-liner hack, 'his pen travelling shrilly over the foolscap'. A harmless enough garrotter who was also a remarkable performer upon the jew's harp.

With the aid now of his lowest of the low assistants, a certain cab-driver is summoned to Baker Street, and Holmes, on the pretext of asking for help with some luggage, claps a pair of handcuffs on him, handcuffs be it said of the latest scientific pattern, a good deal more efficient than those employed at Scotland Yard. The cabby turns out to be a young American, Jefferson Hope. Holmes persuades him, shortly before he succumbs to the aneurysm which had given him the furious nose-bleed that accounted for all the blood at the scene of the crime (hence Holmes's deduction of the florid complexion), to tell the whole story of how he came to put to death the two mysterious victims, malcontent Mormons, one of whom had married by force Hope's fiancée, the beautiful Lucy Ferrier. As Holmes afterwards explained, 'You see, the whole thing is a chain of logical sequences without a break or flaw.'

'It is wonderful,' Watson cried. 'Your merits should be publicly recognized. You should publish an account of the case. If you won't, I will for you.'

'You may do as you like, Doctor. See here! Look at this!'

Holmes passed to Watson the *Echo* of that day with its account of the business, ending 'It is an open secret that the credit of this smart capture belongs entirely to the well-known Scotland Yard officials, Messrs. Lestrade and Gregson. The man was apprehended, it appears, in the rooms of a certain Mr. Sherlock Holmes, who has himself, as an amateur, shown some talent in the detective line. . . .'

A pattern has been established. Many, many times in the years to come we shall read of Holmes allowing the triumphant laurels to be placed on other brows than his. Not for him plaudits, except those discreet and censored accounts he will permit Watson from time to time cautiously to issue. Not for him the vulgar shouts nor any mafficking hero-worship. For him the sober and significant task, success its only reward.

At this point, however, Sherlock Holmes was by no means seen as his age's champion. He had set up as a consulting detective. From the first few cases that university acquaintances and others had brought him he had begun to establish a reputation with the Scotland Yarders and the private inquiry agents as being a useful man to know when rough-and-ready methods did not seem to be producing an answer. It was in this way, for instance, that he had been enabled even before his introduction to Watson to bring to a happy conclusion the business of the Farintosh Tiara. But he was still a figure in the background, and a not too well rewarded one. Yet his time was coming. 'The Hero', trumpeted Thomas Carlyle, 'can be Poet, Prophet, King, Priest or whom you will, according to the kind of world he finds himself born into.'

During the later 1880s Holmes's reputation built up with rapidity. The number of cases he was consulted over grew and grew, and increased in weight. One of the earliest of them Watson called, when a good many years later, owing to the untimely death of a lady to whom a pledge of secrecy had been given, he was free to set it out, 'The Adventure of the Speckled Band'. It is worth discussing at some length, not because of the singular features which made Watson wish to recount it, but because it is one of the first instances we have of Holmes seeing himself as that knight whose task it was to combat ever-encroaching evil. 'Ah me,' he sighed at the early stage of the business when he and he alone had grasped its essential features, 'it's a wicked world, and when a clever man turns his brains to crime it is the worst of all.'

There was never any doubt about the identity of this clever man. He was Dr Grimesby Roylott, last survivor of one of the oldest Saxon families in England, the Roylotts of Stoke Moran, now reduced to a few acres and the old family house itself. To recoup these fortunes, Roylott had taken a medical degree and gone out to 'our Indian possessions'. There he had married the widow of Major-General Stoner of the Bengal Artillery who had since died herself, leaving her twin daughters, now grown up, each with a small personal fortune.

It was one of these girls, Helen, who sought Holmes's assistance, arriving at Baker Street early one morning apparently trembling with cold. 'It is not cold which makes me shiver. . . . It is fear, Mr. Holmes. It is terror.'

Some two years before, it appears, her sister, then about to marry, had died in unaccountable and horrible circumstances. Her sleep over a period had been disturbed by a mysterious low clear whistling. Then, one stormy night with the wind howling and the rain 'beating and splashing against the windows', there had burst forth suddenly a wild scream of terror. Helen Stoner had rushed out of her room just in time to meet her sister before she had collapsed in death with a shriek of 'It was the band! The

Holmes's sitting-room door is dashed open and a huge man frames himself in the aperture. Sidney Paget's view of Dr Grimesby Roylott.

Holmes lashes
furiously at the bell-
pull in Helen Stoner's
room.

speckled band!' Now, within a fortnight of her own marriage,
Helen, who had had to occupy her dead sister's room, had heard
once more that same low clear whistling in the dead of night.

But before Holmes and Watson had had time to do more than
discuss the mystery after their visitor's departure the door of their
sitting-room was suddenly dashed open and 'a huge man framed
himself in the aperture.' Dr Grimesby Roylott. In a moment he
was vociferating insults. 'You are Holmes the meddler. . . .
Holmes the busybody! . . . Holmes the Scotland Yard jack-in-
office.' He had tracked his step-daughter to Baker Street and he
warned Holmes now that he was a dangerous man to fall foul of,
snatching up the poker from the fireplace to prove his point and
bending it instantly into a curve.

Only when the formidable giant had left did Holmes take up
the poker in his turn and with a single sharp effort straighten it
out.

Down at Stoke Moran Holmes arranged with Helen Stoner to
occupy with Watson that night her room next to the one where
Dr Roylott was apt to pace about, his presence declaring itself by
the smell of his strong Indian cigars. There, having penetrated
the neglected gardens prowled by an Indian-imported ape and
cheetah, the two investigators waited in the darkness. Far away

they could hear the deep tones of the parish clock. Twelve it struck. And one. And two. And even three. Then there was a sudden momentary gleam of light high up in the wall above the head of the bed where Roylott's step-daughter should have been sleeping. And soon a sound became audible, 'a very gentle soothing sound like that of a small jet of steam escaping continually from a kettle.'

Holmes instantly struck a match and lashed furiously with his cane at the bell-pull dangling beside the bed. 'You see it, Watson?' he shouted. 'You see it?'

But a dazzled Watson had seen nothing. All he had done was to hear at just that moment a low clear whistling. And then, while Holmes was still gazing fixedly at the small ventilator just at the top of the bell-rope, there came from the far side of the wall, in Watson's words, 'the most horrible cry to which I have ever listened.'

They went next door. Dr Grimesby Roylott, clad in a long grey dressing-gown, his bare ankles protruding beneath and his feet thrust into red heel-less Turkish slippers, was sprawled there dead. And at his brow there was 'a peculiar yellow band with brownish speckles, which seemed to be bound tightly round his head.'

'It was a swamp adder,' Holmes cried, 'the deadliest snake in India.' Dr Roylott had trained the creature to answer to a whistle call. But Holmes, deducing from such clues as the smell of cigar smoke coming into the adjoining room what the evil man's plan must have been, had been too good for him. 'When a doctor does go wrong,' he declared, 'he is the first of criminals. He has nerve and he has knowledge. Palmer and Pritchard were among the heads of their profession. This man strikes even deeper. . . .'

Holmes was now in full cry. In the year 1887 alone he dealt with the Paradol Chamber affair, the business of the Amateur Mendicant Society and the mysterious loss of the barque *Sophy Anderson*, and he was responsible, too, for unravelling the circumstances behind the extraordinary adventures of the Grice Pattersons on the island of Uffa, as well as solving the Camberwell Poisoning case, in which by winding the dead man's watch he was able to prove that he had gone to bed only some two hours before – yet another instance of his way of going to the simple heart of things.

Yet the crown of that *annus mirabilis* was another case, the one which, it would seem, finally established Holmes as his age's champion, the defeating of the colossal schemes of Baron Maupertuis with, as a sort of coda, his bringing to an

EXECUTION

OF

Dr. PRITCHARD,

AT GLASGOW.

By ELECTRIC TELEGRAPH,—GLASGOW, Friday.

This morning, Friday, July 28th, the last dread sentence of the law was carried into effect on the body of Dr. Pritchard, for the wilful murder of his wife and mother-in-law. The prisoner since his condemnation has conducted himself with great calmness, and has, since his confession become more earnest in his religious duties, and paid marked attention to the exhortations of the Rev. R. S. Oldham and other worthy clergymen who have attended him.

The Sheriffs, with their usual attendants arrived at the prison, and immediately visited the wretched culprit in the condemned cell, when he thanked them for the kindness he had received at their hands. After the formalities had been observed of demanding the prisoner into their custody. Calcraft, the executioner was introduced to the prisoner, and the operation of pinioning having been gone through, and the mournful procession having been formed, began to move towards the scaffold, the chaplain reading the burial service for the dead. The prisoner ascended the scaffold with a firm step, and directly the wretched man appeared, loud murmurs was heard from the vast multitude assembled. Calcraft having adjusted the rope, and drew the cap over his eyes, the signal was given, the bolt withdrawn, and the wretched man, after struggling for a few moments, ceased to exist.

extraordinarily swift conclusion, even though he was still recovering from the complete exhaustion which his efforts had brought on, the adventure of the Reigate Squires.

The Maupertuis conspiracy and the whole question of the Netherlands-Sumatra Company, that intermingling of the worst in politics and finance, took Holmes two months of unremitting work to resolve, work which more than once – how this would have delighted old Thomas Carlyle – kept him awake and active for five days at a stretch. But the details of the affair are not, even today, at our disposal. Such of them as must have surfaced in the world's Press cannot be traced back to the parent wrongdoing, and Watson left no connected account. We can get some idea of its scale and possible consequences only by looking at another narrowly averted financial holocaust, though one without a background of fraud if not lacking in those other necessary elements, greed and recklessness. This was the failure of Baring's Bank, one of the great houses of the City of London, just a few years later, in 1890.

The two years preceding this resounding failure had been a period of grabbing boom, an ugly symptom of the declining times. In South Africa the Rand goldfields had suddenly increased output. Simultaneously in South America there was the culmination of years of spend, spend, spend, with Argentina's public debt, as one instance, rising from a modest ten millions in 1875 to seventy millions in 1889, a large part of the borrowings being used to buy goods from the churning manufactories of Britain. Holmes, indeed, during the minor affair of the Stockbroker's Clerk in 1889, encountered young Mr Hall Pycroft who had just lost 'a billet at Coxon and Woodhouse, of Drapers' Gardens, but they were let in early in the spring through the Venezuelan loan'.

In this atmosphere of easy pickings even the great House of Baring's had over-speculated, incurring liabilities which they were unable to honour amounting to no less than £21,000,000, a huge enough sum in terms of the last quarter of the twentieth century, an immense one in the last quarter of the nineteenth. But while the situation was still secret William Lidderdale, the Governor of the Bank of England, was told the facts. He acted then as swiftly and almost as tirelessly as Holmes had done in the Netherlands-Sumatra affair, though he had no criminal mind to combat. He sold Exchequer bonds to Russia and obtained £1,500,000 in gold. He borrowed £3,000,000 from the Bank of France. From the joint-stock banks in London he raised within eighteen hours a guarantee of another £7,000,000. And thus he

William Lidderdale.

averted a panic liquidation which would have struck deep at the foundations of trade and industry through all Great Britain.

Lidderdale's name has gone down in the history books, if chiefly those of economic history. Holmes's struggle in his single combat with that unscrupulous genius Baron Maupertuis should have entitled him to a similar fame. But fame, as far as he could, Holmes eschewed, and the full details of that engagement are lost for ever. But the people whom he saved from ruin were not ungrateful. When Dr Watson hurried across to France to find Holmes lying in a state of exhaustion in a hotel room in Lyons the floor was 'literally ankle-deep in congratulatory telegrams'.

When Holmes had fully recovered there came the Darlington Substitution scandal, the affair at Arnsworth Castle and the Dundas Separation case as well as the business to which Watson gave the title 'A Case of Identity' and the matter in which Holmes was able to be of assistance to the King of Scandinavia.

None of those cases is without interest, but another Watson chronicle is worth examining at greater length next for the light it throws on the aims and motives of the ever-reticent Holmes. This is the adventure Watson called 'The Resident Patient'. In itself it was a comparatively simple affair, though not without its *outré* details. There was, for instance, the moment when Holmes and Watson found the corpulent man calling himself Blessington, who had bought and furnished a house in fashionable Brook Street for young Dr Percy Trevelyan, hanging from a lamp-hook, his neck 'drawn out like a plucked chicken's, making the rest of him seem the more obese and unnatural by contrast', having apparently committed suicide. By a minute

Watson in a brown study, as imagined by Sidney Paget.

study of footprints Holmes was able to show the death was murder, and a brief consultation of Scotland Yard records was enough for him to identify the mysterious Blessington as a notorious bank-robber who had betrayed his associates and had at last suffered at their hands.

However, before Dr Trevelyan's arrival at 221B Baker Street Watson tells us that Holmes had, teasingly, been giving him a demonstration of his power of reconstructing a chain of thought in some other person's head, an ability he shared with the extraordinary Chevalier Dupin of whom Edgar Allan Poe wrote. And Watson's particular 'brown study' had begun when he had glanced at one of two pictures he had recently acquired to embellish their rooms, a portrait of General Gordon.

The choice of subject tells us a good deal. General Gordon, 'Chinese' Gordon, was one of the great heroes of the Victorian public. As a simple major, aged twenty-seven, he had gone on detachment in the early 1860s to command a Chinese army and, thanks largely to the force of his own personality, had crushed a rebellion which had at one time seemed to threaten the Emperor's very throne. It is an early sign, incidentally, of Britain's soon-to-be-overweening pride that Gordon had gone to China originally to join a punitive force sent out after the Chinese had seized a British ship they suspected of having a cargo of opium.

Nor did Gordon's heroism end with China. He was pushed aside for a good many years by Army chiefs suspicious of a man who was at the least an oddity, preferring any life away from civilization to the social round at home besides being a religious enthusiast of a fervently missionary kind. But in 1874, as the result of a chance encounter with the Khedive of Egypt, he was invited to become Governor of Equatoria, Egypt's southern Sudan province, a thankless appointment in which he strove to put down a brutal slave trade, and he later became Governor-General of all Sudan. However, this experience made him the right man in 1884 to be given command, by the Prime Minister, Gladstone, himself, of a force charged with evacuating Europeans from the Sudan when the rebel chief, el Mahdi, had run riot there. But in Khartoum Gordon found himself surrounded and, with a relief column approaching too slowly, met his death, to be hailed at home more loudly than ever before as a supreme hero.

Only in neighbouring Abyssinia did the French poet-turned-trader, Arthur Rimbaud, comment bitterly: 'After this it will be the English, and the English alone, who will be crippling the safety of every business enterprise along the coast with their ridiculous political play-acting.' Queen Victoria, writing to Gordon's sister, spoke of 'your dear, noble, heroic brother' and Gladstone, whose Ministry was toppled partly as a result of the general outcry, called the martyr 'a hero of heroes'.

So there were portraits a-plenty to be had when a year or so later Watson decided that the Baker Street rooms needed a picture or two to counterbalance his friend's criminal likenesses. But his choice of Gordon, with Holmes's tacit approval, had a more particular significance. The similarities between the hero of China and Khartoum and the first consulting detective were close indeed.

Gordon, like Holmes, was a man of almost obsessional modesty who yet had a startlingly high opinion of himself. At the height of his first fame he insisted that his return from China should be in the greatest secrecy to avoid any reception on his arrival, sending a cryptic message to his mother, 'the individual is coming home.' Yet at the same time he had gone to extreme lengths to make sure the Emperor awarded him the coveted Yellow Jacket of which no more than forty could be bestowed. Again, in Africa, when after overcoming enormous obstacles he got a steamer launched on unexplored Lake Albert Nyanza, 'to give practical proof of what I think is the inordinate praise which is given to an explorer' he left to a lieutenant the renown of being the first to navigate those waters. Retiring though he was, however, he shared with Holmes all the dash and energy and love of danger that were the marks of the English gentleman.

But, like the Holmes whom Watson had noted as lazing 'for days on end' on the sofa, Gordon too could have spells of almost totally opting-out. In Equatoria, when once there was acute danger of an attack on his camp and his deputy dared to ignore the hatchet placed as a 'keep out' sign at his tent door, Gordon was found sitting with in front of him an open Bible and an equally open bottle of brandy and would say nothing more than 'You are commander of the camp.'

If Gordon from time to time succumbed to the brandy bottle, Watson was to find before he had been long acquainted with Holmes that his paragon was all too apt, in moments of boredom, to resort to hypodermic injections of cocaine or morphine. If it can be said that the English gentleman of that era could be likened to the loyal, brave and manly dog – and how the Victorians cherished their dogs, and how often do we find the faithful creatures weaving their way through the Holmes annals – then, although Holmes exemplified all of those qualities, he had too a good deal about him of the cat. When later we shall find him living rough on Dartmoor in the Baskerville business 'he had contrived', Watson says, 'with that cat-like love of personal cleanliness which was one of his characteristics, that his chin should be as smooth and his linen as perfect as if he were in Baker Street' and elsewhere he speaks of 'one of his quick, feline pounces'. Gordon showed many signs, too, of having to suppress secret sexual longings, and there are similar hints to be taken up in the life of Sherlock Holmes.

Finally, like Holmes, the total bachelor and furious devotee (outside his periods of moody idleness) to work, bachelor Gordon would often quote the Scripture, 'To each is allotted a distinct work', and he would toil, too, regardless of reward, reducing his own salary on his appointment to Equatoria from £10,000 to £2,000. Holmes, equally, we shall see spurning large sums once his modest needs are satisfied. And one last comparison. Both men hated dining out. 'Men think giving dinners is conferring a favour on you,' snarled Gordon. 'Why not give dinners to those who need them?' And Holmes, almost as abrasive, spoke of 'those unwelcome social summonses which call upon a man either to be bored or to lie.'

But Watson had another new picture in mind for their walls. Beside his just-framed portrait of Gordon there leant an as yet unframed one, of Henry Ward Beecher. Another figure of contradiction here. Beecher was perhaps the foremost American pulpit-star of his time, and like his sister Harriet Beecher Stowe, authoress of *Uncle Tom's Cabin*, and General Gordon, a vigorous

Above: General Gordon.

Above right: Henry Ward Beecher.

Right: Harriet Beecher Stowe.

opponent of slavery. In 1863, when the cause of the slave-owning South was regarded in Establishment circles in Britain as a praiseworthy movement of national self-determination on a par with Byron's Greece of forty years before, Beecher had come to England to give a series of pro-Northern lectures which were, in Holmes's words, not well received 'by the more turbulent of our people', to Watson's passionate indignation.

So here was America, not for the first time or the last, pushing its way into the English pattern of Holmes's life. It has been calculated, indeed, that one in five of the cases Watson described has some reference to America, though they tend to cluster late in the saga as, with the stately edifice of High Victorian England crumbling ever faster, the new and newly-rich country across the Atlantic claimed more and more attention. But here we see America as a cauldron of troubles, as already it has seemed with the eruption into London life of Jefferson Hope's Mormon victims of *A Study in Scarlet*, for in those days the Mormons, even the best of them, appeared to be direly revolutionary.

Before long Holmes was to encounter two other cases where violent America played a major part. There was the affair of the Five Orange Pips in which the Ku Klux Klan, that 'terrible secret society' whose name derived 'from a fanciful resemblance to the sound produced by cocking a rifle' came to the quiet Sussex town of Horsham. And there was the case of the Noble Bachelor, a less alarming affair in which the young American

A Ku Klux Klan meeting: an early photograph.

The rough and tumble of gold prospecting in
America in 1880. A contemporary drawing.

Lord Robert St Simon,
as Sidney Paget saw him.

bride of the somewhat pettish Lord St Simon disappeared from
the wedding breakfast, an action that proved to have its origins
in a rough-and-tumble Rocky Mountains gold-prospecting
camp. It was at the conclusion of that business that Holmes, with
stately Victorian hauteur, suggested that the *enfant terrible* nation
would be better back with Mamma's apron-strings. 'I am one of
those who believe that the folly of a monarch and the blundering
of a Minister in far gone years will not prevent our children from
being some day citizens of the same world-wide country. . . .'

In the course of that case, too, Holmes showed his
acquaintance with the great American writer-naturalist H.D.
Thoreau, quoting his remark about circumstantial evidence
(some of it is very convincing, 'as when you find a trout in the
milk'). Thoreau, the thinker who first pointed out to us that 'the
mass of men lead lives of quiet desperation', seems at first sight an
odd writer for Holmes to quote, a disturber from America, if of
a different sort, a drop-out from the urgent concerns of the

57

H.D. Thoreau.

nineteenth century, a quiet resister who was to have not a little
influence on the movements away from what the great Age of
Victoria most firmly believed in. But Holmes was never as simple
a figure, nor as simple a fighter, as on the surface he appeared to
be.

Yet Henry Ward Beecher, preacher whose portrait was to
adorn Holmes's walls, flag-bearer in the anti-slavery movement,
like Thoreau, and a champion, too, with his 1885 book *Evolution
and Religion*, of the Darwinian theory which Holmes equally
believed in yet which had, nevertheless, been such a hammer
stroke to the established order, had another side to his character.
After several years of ugly rumour, in 1874 he was accused in a
spectacular law case that travelled even across the broad
Atlantic of committing adultery with the wife of one of his
friends, the jury eventually failing to agree. Not then an
unambiguously heroic figure to look down daily on Sherlock
Holmes.

But, whatever thoughts these two portraits brought to
Holmes's mind in his darker hours, outwardly he had now
attained a pinnacle. His reputation reached to the highest places
in the land, as is shown by 'The Adventure of the Second Stain',
a case which Watson was not to put before the public till many
years later. At its start, we hear, the humble rooms in Baker
Street welcomed two visitors of European fame, Lord Bellinger,
twice Prime Minister, 'high-nosed, eagle-eyed and dominant',
and the Right Honourable Trelawney Hope, 'hardly yet of
middle age and endowed with every beauty of body and of
mind', Secretary of State for European Affairs. They explained

to Holmes that an indiscreet letter from a foreign potentate had
mysteriously disappeared from a locked despatch-box, a letter
which on second thoughts its writer would wish to withdraw
since if published anywhere it would so inflame British public
opinion – bellicose Britain now – that within a week the country
would be involved in a great war.

Holmes begins his task here by looking at the three heads in
London of the profession of international spy or secret agent, the
names of all that fraternity being now, as he says, 'tolerably
familiar to me'. Again we see him taking up arms against forces
working in hiding for the overthrow of the status quo. It is a front
in his ceaseless war on which he was to fight again and again.
Indeed two of the three men he named here he would investigate
once more nearly ten years later when he suspected they were
waiting to receive, not the dangerous document he was at
present searching for, but the plans of the Bruce-Partington
submarine, the vessel which should retain for his country her
naval superiority in the war that by then had begun to get close

Two visitors to Baker
Street, the Rt Hon.
Trelawney Hope and
eagle-eyed Lord
Bellinger.

One of the many rival contenders in the new art of submarine warfare, a vessel doubtless to be outdone by the Bruce-Partington craft, the plans for which only Sherlock Holmes could recover. An *Illustrated London News* engraving.

with renascent, organized, science-based Germany. In that adventure 'numerous small fry' were set aside as the agent likely to buy the plans in favour of either Adolph Meyer, of 13 Great George Street, Westminster, or Louis La Rothiere, of Campden Mansions, Notting Hill, or Hugo Oberstein, of Caulfield Gardens, Kensington. In this affair he adds to La Rothiere and Oberstein one Eduardo Lucas, of 16 Godolphin Street, Westminster. The very presence of such men in London, sitting crouched waiting to purchase whatever secrets come the way of greedy petty traitors, shows graphically the creeping rottenness spreading into the sound body of England.

But the Second Stain case proves not to be an affair of venality, unlike the Bruce-Partington one ten sliding years on when the brother of Sir James Walter, the naval engineer 'whose decorations and sub-titles fill two lines of a book of reference', a Colonel in the British Army, was found to have a Stock Exchange debt far beyond his capabilities and earned finally from Holmes that terrible rebuke, 'How an English gentleman could behave in such a manner . . .'.

Here Holmes discovers, thanks to observing that a stain on a carpet does not correspond with the mark on the floor beneath, that Eduardo Lucas had obtained the dangerous letter by a mixture of blackmail and deception from none other than the European Secretary's wife and that she had with great spirit retrieved it in advance of his own discoveries from Lucas's house when he had chanced to be murdered by a discarded mistress 'of Creole origin'. Holmes in the end exonerates Lady Hilda Trelawney Hope and contrives to pretend to her husband, if not altogether to the eagle-eyed Prime Minister, that the missing document had simply become tucked away with others in the dispatch-box.

A figure high in the counsels of the nation protected from a falsely based scandal. In another case at about this time it was a person of considerably lower standing whom Holmes protected from a different, if equally false, scandal, a certain Major Prendergast wrongfully accused of cheating at the Tankerville card-club. This, again, is an affair of which we cannot know any details since Watson does no more than mention it. But it is a sign of its times. A very similar case did indeed come to the courts at about this period, the so-called 'Tranby Croft affair' of 1891. And that was a business which brought into the witness-box no less a person than Edward, Prince of Wales, heir to the throne, a man who was to epitomize in many ways the new, noisier, more vulgar, less decent world which Holmes fought to hold back over the years, and in the end fought in vain.

The heir to the throne in court as a result of playing baccarat, an illegal gambling game, and a member of his close circle, Lieutenant-Colonel Sir William Gordon Cumming, seeking in a

Holmes observes the misplaced second stain, in the case to which Watson gave that name.

The Tranby Croft Case. *Left*, The Prince of Wales in the box; *right*, the Judge, Lord Coleridge; and, *far right*, a juryman daring enough to ask His Royal Highness a question. An *Illustrated London News* artist's court sketches.

libel action to repel an accusation of cheating. The heir to the throne, next to the Queen herself an intended example to the nation, failing to report the matter as dishonourable conduct by a fellow officer as was his duty under Queen's Regulations and having to apologize to Parliament for his failure. A German newspaper cartoon punning on the royal motto *Ich Dien*, 'I serve' as 'I deal'. The heir to the throne later taking one of his many holidays at the spa of Marienbad and inviting a lady to join him at cards only for her to decline with 'Sir, I do not know a king from a knave.' How far down had things gone from the days of not so many years before.

Nor was this the first time that Edward, Prince of Wales, known to his intimates as Tum-Tum, had been a witness in an unpleasant court case. In 1871 a Sir Charles Mordaunt had sought a divorce from his twenty-one-year-old wife, citing two of the Prince's circle as co-respondents. But the lady had claimed that the child she had borne was the result of having 'done wrong' with, among others, the Prince himself. So the Prince then had had to go into the box. This case, however, was in the days when it was still felt to be vital to avoid open scandal, and the Prince had made no more than a seven-minute appearance,

simply denying any suggestion of adultery, and no cross-examination had followed.

But court appearances were only the iceberg tips of a life that was rapidly becoming notorious. It was a life, too, that showed few signs of that industrious application to the allotted task which was so much a mark of the Prince's mother and of her age, and not a little, too, of Sherlock Holmes. But, as the Queen herself said of her son, 'newspapers and very rarely a novel are all he reads' and indeed even in the newspaper line it was not *The Times* he chose but gossip-crammed *Reynolds News*, founded by the soft pornographer G. W. M. Reynolds, author of *Mysteries of the Inquisition*, *Mysteries of the Courts of London*, etc.

In the words of the contemporary poet and diarist, Wilfrid Scawen Blunt, the Prince had as well a 'passion for pageantry and ceremonial and dressing up' and 'was never tired of ... cattle shows and rabbit shows and shows of every kind, while every night of his life he was to be seen at theatres, operas and music halls.' Shooting, too, took up an extraordinary amount of time and energy. The game book at his Sandringham house records for the season of 1896–97 a bag of 13,958 pheasants, 3,965 partridge, 6,185 rabbits, 836 hares, 271 duck, 77 woodcock,

'Everyone comments on *my* simplicity.' Queen Victoria writes a letter.

52 teal, 18 pigeons, 8 snipe and 27 'various'. Nor in this round of entertainments were Sundays sacred. At his London home, Marlborough House, dinner-parties began to be given on that once hushed evening.

But these perhaps were only a symptom of the time. In 1886 the publishers' lists had novels in pride of place with 969 new titles compared with religion's 752.

Nor were shooting on an immense scale and Sunday dinner-parties the end of the Prince's diversions. Despite a specific injunction in the rules which his father Prince Albert, Albert the Good, had laid down for him when he had come of age that his conduct must never include 'anything approaching a practical joke', the weaker members of his circle could expect continually to be tripped into baths of cold water, to have brandy poured slowly over their heads, to find live rabbits or dead birds in their beds, to have the tips of burning cigars pressed into their palms amid loud guffaws all round. As early as 1869, indeed, his mother had felt compelled to say to him about the example he was setting, 'There is a *very* strong feeling against the luxuriousness

Right: A passion for pageantry and ceremonial and dressing up. The Prince of Wales leads the Household Cavalry in review before his mother.

Below: His Royal Highness 'Tum-Tum' and feathered friends.

and frivolity of society – and everyone comments on *my* simplicity.' Some pomposity, no doubt, in those underlinings, but it does not detract from the Queen's very real point. A heavy frivolity, luxury and money were what Prince Edward, Tum-Tum, stood for.

One day the stern *Times* was to say of him tactfully, 'If he had been born in a humbler station he might have made a very successful businessman.' He certainly loved money, its getting and spending, and it was alleged that when he came at last to the throne those financiers who had paid off his enormous debts were awarded knighthoods.

It was debts such as those that were to bring Sherlock Holmes and Edward, Prince of Wales, first into contact, if only at second hand. One bright crisp February morning, Watson tells us, as he looked out of the Baker Street windows at the snow 'ploughed into a brown crumbly band by the traffic' (brown, of course, with horse droppings), he saw a man hurrying towards the house in a state of almost comic contortion, despite 'black frock-coat, shining hat, neat brown gaiters and well-cut pearl-grey trousers.'

'After many other curious, lamentable and delectable adventures, Edwardysseus is washed ashore on his own island. To him appears, in the guise of a Highland shepherd, his mother, Pallas Victoria, and puts him on his way.' Max Beerbohm's view of the relationship between Queen and Royal heir.

He proved to be Alexander Holder of the banking firm of Holder & Stevenson, Threadneedle Street. The previous day, he says, 'I was seated in my office at the Bank, when a card was brought in to me by one of the clerks. I started when I saw the name, for it was that of none other than – well, perhaps even to you I had better say no more than that it was a name which is a household word all over the earth – one of the highest, noblest, most exalted names in England.' We can have little doubt whom this heavy circumlocution disguises.

'Mr Holder,' the exalted person began immediately, 'I have been informed that you are in the habit of advancing money.'

'The firm do so when the security is good.'

'It is absolutely essential to me that I should have fifty thousand pounds at once. I could of course borrow so trifling a sum ten times over from my friends, but I much prefer to make it a matter of business. . . .'

And within a few minutes the visitor had his loan until the following Monday, and Mr Holder had as security 'one of the most precious public possessions of the Empire', the Beryl Coronet. Only, hapless fellow, to find that night his somewhat spendthrift son standing beside his opened bureau with in his hands the precious object, from which were missing three of its thirty-nine jewels.

Mr Alexander Holder, of the banking firm of Holder and Stevenson, Threadneedle Street, is calmed by Sherlock Holmes. Illustration by Sidney Paget.

Holmes quite rapidly, by observation and deduction from footprints at the scene and by adhering to 'an old maxim of mine that when you have excluded the impossible, whatever remains, however improbable, must be the truth', gets to the root of the mystery. The boy had only been protecting his girl cousin who had fallen prey to the vicious Sir George Burnwell, 'one of the most dangerous men in England'. By clapping a pistol to the head of this villain when he had snatched a life-preserver from the wall, Holmes was able to recover the missing stones and make sure all ended well, even for the man who had such a pressing need for £50,000 over the week-end.

Victorian life-preservers.

A good many years later, in the September of 1902 when Edward, Prince of Wales, had become His Majesty King Edward VII, Emperor of India, Defender of the Faith, Holmes had another indirect encounter with him. Watson aptly entitles the business 'The Adventure of the Illustrious Client'. Holmes was approached to take up the case in the most circuitous of ways.

Watson recounts that, as early one afternoon they were lying at ease in the Northumberland Avenue Turkish baths, a relaxation for which they both had a weakness, Holmes took a note from the pocket of his coat and invited him to read it.

> *Sir James Damery presents his compliments to Mr Sherlock Holmes and will call upon him at 4.30 to-morrow. Sir James begs to say that the matter upon which he desires to consult Mr Holmes is very delicate, and also very important. He trusts, therefore, that Mr Holmes will make every effort to grant this interview, and that he will confirm it over the telephone to the Carlton Club.*

Gone, we see, is the heyday of the telegram, Holmes's favourite means of communication, stately even at its most urgent: we are in the era of the insistent, jabbering telephone. And even Holmes has to make use of it.

Sir James, when he comes to Baker Street, impresses the ever-credulous Watson with his 'lucent top-hat' and the pearl pin in his black satin cravat, but less so Sherlock Holmes. When told he

will be facing an individual than whom 'there is no more dangerous man in Europe', Holmes replies with a smile, 'I have had several opponents to whom that flattering term has been applied', adding as a small snub to a visitor who has retained all the while his white kid gloves, 'Don't you smoke? Then you will excuse me if I light my pipe.' We may imagine he chose the vicious shag he occasionally favoured, a tobacco manufactured (said a Victorian expert) 'of the strongest and very worst kind of leaf', though Thackeray and Tennyson are reported to have smoked it once while discussing the poetry of Elizabeth Barrett Browning.

Sir James tells Holmes he will be up against a certain Baron Gruner.

'You mean the Austrian murderer?'

Sir James, Watson says, threw up his kid-gloved hands with a laugh. 'There is no getting past you, Mr Holmes!'

The Baron, it appears, has got into his toils Violet, daughter of General de Merville, of Khyber fame – how our Indian

Turkish baths, a relaxation for which both Holmes and Watson had a weakness. A contemporary photograph of the cool-room at the Jermyn Street establishment.

Opposite:
The Carlton Club in 1890.

Sir James threw up his kid-gloved hands with a laugh. 'There is no getting past you, Mr Holmes.' Howard Elcock's illustration.

possessions enter in at every chink – a girl whom Damery describes as 'young, rich, beautiful, accomplished, a wonder-woman in every way.' But the General is not the client. Instead it is 'one who has known the General for many years and taken a paternal interest in this young girl since she wore short frocks.' We may ask, I think, whether the General was in earlier days a crony of H.R.H. Tum-Tum, one of the baccarat circle, or whether when Violet de Merville grew out of her short frocks an eye that was ever ready to look at a pretty woman lingered long on her perhaps during another Mediterranean yachting trip like the one on which she fell in love with Gruner.

Damery concludes by asking Holmes, as a point of honour, not to break in on his client's incognito. Holmes gave a whimsical smile, we are told. 'I think I may safely promise that.'

But we may be sure it was the opponent and not the client that decided Holmes to take up the case despite his earlier assertion that he could not work with a mystery at both ends of the matter. And Gruner proves a formidable enemy indeed. Before their struggle is over Holmes has been set on outside the Café Royal and badly injured – though not so badly as he allows Baron Gruner to suppose. And in the end it is not without burgling the Baron's luxurious house, 'built by a South African gold king in the days of the great boom', that he contrives his enemy's downfall.

But the intrusion into Holmes's fought-for world of the royal Tum-Tum, that figure of aggressive blatancy – 'rather inclined to be noisy,' drily commented the novelist and military historian, Sir Arthur Conan Doyle, after sitting next to him – has sent us ahead of ourselves. We must go back now to the late 1880s. Here we find Holmes both enormously busy and much more engaged with high affairs.

Not that he was invariably successful. He triumphed certainly in the extremely complex affair Watson called *The Valley of Fear*, initially by his skill in solving a cryptogram – he was the author of

Outside the Café Royal, scene of the assault on Holmes by Baron Gruner's bully-boys. A photograph of the period.

But Holmes is much less hurt than he allows his opponent to believe.

'a trifling monograph on the subject, in which I analyse one hundred and sixty separate ciphers' – a code which made use of *Whitaker's Almanack*, not as Watson suggested *Bradshaw's Guide*, that indispensable key to the complexities of the Victorian railway systems with its vocabulary, in Holmes's words, 'nervous and terse, but limited'. And then by sharp observation linked to remorseless deduction he was able to show that the murderer of the dead American lying in his study in moat-encircled Birlstone Manor was none other than the American himself, a man of honour pursued by the vicious, anarchist Scowrers of the Pennsylvania coalfields, an organization much akin to the Irish secret society the Molly Maguires, originally formed to resist paying rents and later in America a tough organization of trade-union terrorists.

In the course of his long battles Holmes was to find himself face to face more than once with conspiratorial secret societies. They constituted another front in his many-sided war. Not only was there the American Ku Klux Klan as well as the Mormons, but in later years there was the Red Circle, in the strange case to which Watson gave that name, with its tentacles stretching from Italy to New York and on to London, and there was the equally Italian Mafia in the background of the Six Napoleons affair, while in the Golden Pince-Nez case it was the Russian Nihilists.

In the matter of 'The Yellow Face', however, when Holmes had forced his way into a cottage in the quiet suburb of Norbury he found, not the villainy or even devilry he was expecting, but only a widowed American lady with her little masked coal-black daughter. It was then that he said to Watson, 'if it should ever strike you that I am getting a little over-confident in my powers, or giving less pains to a case than it deserves, kindly whisper "Norbury" in my ear, and I shall be infinitely obliged to you.'

Then among the failures there was the adventure of 'A Scandal in Bohemia'. It was in this that Holmes came up against an adversary, among all the men of immense evil he encountered from Baron Maupertuis to Dr Grimesby Roylott, from Sir George Burnwell to Baron Gruner and worse, to whom he was in the end happy to give best. 'To Sherlock Holmes,' Watson begins his account, 'she was always *the* woman.' Irene Adler, 'the well-known adventuress', born in America, a contralto at La Scala, prima donna until her retirement of the Imperial Opera of Warsaw, before many years have elapsed to be the late Irene Adler: Holmes was to keep on his watch-chain for the remainder of his life a sovereign she bestowed on him in the course of their encounter.

Opposite: Holmes tackles the cipher that began the Valley of Fear case.

Sherlock Holmes, master of disguise, in the likeness of a drunken-looking groom, and in the character of an amiable and simple-minded non-conformist clergyman. Paget's illustrations for *A Scandal in Bohemia*.

The clash is simply enough described. Into the Baker Street rooms on the night of 20 March 1888 there irrupted a hugely tall, immensely richly dressed man, stately of bearing, wearing a small mask. Before long Holmes has made him admit he is Wilhelm Gottsreich Sigismond von Ormstein, Grand Duke of Cassel-Falstein and hereditary King of Bohemia. He has come, he says, 'incognito from Prague for the purpose of consulting you.' It seems he has committed an indiscretion with Irene Adler, leaving in her possession some letters and a photograph which she now threatens to send to his fiancée, Clotilde Lothman von Saxe-Meningen.

Holmes, who was always a master of disguise, able on occasion to deceive, close to, even Watson, reconnoitres in the likeness of a drunken-looking groom the house, Briony Lodge, in St John's Wood where the lady is living, only to find himself co-opted as a

'Good-night, Mr Sherlock Holmes': drawing by Sidney Paget.

witness to her marriage with an English barrister, receiving that sovereign for his pains. Next, disguised in the character of an amiable and simple-minded Nonconformist clergyman, he succeeds by a simple ruse in locating the actual hiding-place of the papers. He promises himself now that next day he will show King Wilhelm where they are.

But. But, as with Watson Holmes goes back in at the door of 221B, a voice calls out in the darkness, 'Good night, Mr Sherlock Holmes.' It appears to come from a slim youth in an ulster hurrying by, and when next day they call at Briony Lodge it is to find in the hiding-place only a note, saying that the compromising letters will not now be used, together with an innocent photograph. This latter Holmes begs in place of the emerald snake-ring the King offers him, a second memento of a boy-player mistress of disguise.

Holmes seemed never to wish to have a relationship with a woman more direct than that of cherishing these two keepsakes. 'Women are never entirely to be trusted,' he said to Watson a few months later in the course of the case called *The Sign of Four* and, in telling the adventure of the Dying Detective, Watson will say of him plainly, 'He disliked and distrusted the sex', while he is even more outspoken during the Greek Interpreter case in speaking of 'his aversion to women'. Nevertheless it is in the same passage that Watson notes that his friend 'had a remarkable gentleness and courtesy' in dealing with the opposite sex.

If Holmes were a man of the late twentieth century we could hardly fail to conclude from this evidence that his sexual drive was directed to the male, to wonder indeed to what extent it actually would manifest itself and even, sinking to the gossipiest speculation, to hazard conjectures about the *ménage à deux* at 221B Baker Street, especially when we remember that so taboo was the subject then that the word 'homosexuality' did not appear in print until 1897. But Holmes was a man of the nineteenth century, a Victorian to the bone, and, hard though it may be to believe nowadays, I think it is clear that the middle- and upper-class Victorian Englishman did often contrive to sink his sexual energies to an extent which in the sex-obsessed 1970s we find hard to credit. Yet the Victorians, after all, were not bombarded as we are with sexual propaganda of every sort from underwear advertisements to semi-learned pleas for the importance of the orgasm. Long skirts and stiffly buttoned frock-coats, the absence of titillation in any openly obtainable reading matter must all have made a life of abstinence much easier.

But there were, of course, exceptions, and among women as well as men. With the advance of the years Holmes was to meet at least one other adventuress besides Irene Adler. She was Madame Isadora Klein in the case of the Three Gables, the Pernambuco-born widow of the German sugar king – see here again the rise of Germany in the thrusting of the nations, the arrogance of new wealth – of whom Watson said, 'So roguish and exquisite did she look . . . that I felt that of all Holmes's criminals this was the one whom he would find it hardest to face.' However Holmes proved immune, when it came to it, to sentiment.

Yet adventuresses continued to be exceptions. For the most part Society still insisted that a woman must not 'stray' and even that a man who was too openly seen to do so must be punished. Thus the politician Charles Dilke, once thought of as a future Prime Minister, was forced to quit Parliament altogether in 1886 because his sexual conduct was spoken of in detail in a divorce

Right:
Winwood Reade.

Below:
Charles Stewart Parnell.

Below right:
Sir Charles Dilke.

action, and four years later Parnell, the uncrowned king of Ireland, was to have his power at Westminster broken because of his liaison with Mrs Kitty O'Shea. The position of women at that time is well illustrated in a book Holmes recommended to Watson in the course of *The Sign of Four* case as 'one of the most remarkable ever penned', *The Martyrdom of Man* by Winwood Reade, a sort of nineteenth-century equivalent in its large rhetorical optimism to the books of Teilhard de Chardin. It came out in 1872 with enormous success, including a direct recommendation in a speech by Gladstone. This is what Holmes would have read about women in it:

> The abhorrence of the impure, the sense of duty, the fear of punishment, all unite and form a moral law which women themselves enforce, becoming the guardians of their own honour, and treating as a traitor to her sex the woman who betrays her trust. For her the most compassionate have no mercy; she has broken those laws of honour on which society is founded. It is forbidden to receive her; it is an insult to women to allude to her existence, to pronounce her name. She is condemned without inquiry, as the officer is condemned who had shown cowardice before the foe. For the life of women is a battle-field: virtue is their courage and peace of mind their reward. It is certainly an extraordinary fact that women should be subjected to a severe social discipline from which men are almost entirely exempt. As we have shown, it is to be explained by history; it is due to the ancient subjection of woman to man. But it is not the women who are to be pitied: it is they who alone are free, for by that discipline they are preserved from the tyranny of vice.

The Sign of Four case – it was of all Holmes's adventures the one most intimately to affect his Boswell, since during it he met his future wife – provides another illustration of the position of women in Sherlock Holmes's world. His client in the affair, Miss Mary Morstan, Watson's wife-to-be, was a governess.

Ever since in the pattern of society the concept of 'the lady' had become clear, someone apart from the coarse majority of her sex, a fit companion only for 'the gentleman', a considerable complication had existed: inevitably there came to be some daughters of gentlemen without adequate means of support. There were the girls from the poorer parsonages, or girls, like Mary Morstan, whose fathers, generally younger sons, had died before earning a competence. In Miss Morstan's case, in fact, her father, an officer in an Indian Army Regiment, had disappeared mysteriously ten years before on his first night back in England.

For all ladies without the means to live a lady's life almost only one possibility was open, a position as a governess. In Yorkshire

The Governess, from an article
on the occupation in the
Illustrated London News of 1880.

in the early part of the century the daughters of the Reverend
Patrick Brontë had endured this life, and written about it. But
they are only the best known of thousands. And 'endure' is the
word for the life. Removed from the servants of a household by
an impassable social ditch, often disdained by their supposed
social equals from financial snobbery, their days were frequently
lonely and hard. Thackeray said it for all of them: 'She sits alone
in the schoolroom, high, high up in the lone house, when the
little ones are long since asleep, before her dismal little tea-tray,
and her little desk, containing her mother's letters and her
mementoes of home.'

In such a position, too, the poor creatures were open to all sorts
of abuses. Seduction by a grown-up son of the house was not
uncommon. That ranger through the sexual undergrowth of
Victorian society, the pseudonymous 'Walter', encountered
more than a few prostitutes who had been governesses in this
situation. Or they might be obliged to carry out orders as curious
as those imposed on Miss Violet Hunter, whom Holmes aided in
the Copper Beeches case, being ordered to sit at a particular

window wearing a cast-off dress, to cut her hair short, to make a favourite of a nauseating little boy. 'Oh,' said his father, 'if you could see him killing cockroaches with a slipper! Smack! Smack! Smack!' And all this isolated in a remote house in the country where – we have Holmes's words for it – 'It is my belief, Watson, founded upon experience, that the lowest and vilest alleys in London do not present a more dreadful record of sin than does the smiling and beautiful countryside.'

'If you could see him killing cockroaches with a slipper!' Illustration by G. Fonseca to a French translation of Watson's account of the Copper Beeches case.

Women by the thousand were caught in such traps by the laws of Victorian society, caught fast as was Miss Hunter until Holmes saw that she was being tricked into impersonating her employer's step-daughter to prevent a marriage that would deprive him of the use of her fortune. Or caught in the gentle trap which held Mary Morstan, the home of the kindly Mrs Cecil Forrester.

Miss Morstan had come to Holmes when she had received an anonymous letter telling her that she was a wronged woman and asking her to keep a rendezvous, to which she might bring two protectors, 'at the third pillar from the left outside the Lyceum Theatre tonight at seven o'clock'. Holmes analyses the handwriting in this letter: 'There is vacillation in his k's and self-esteem in his capitals.' And then, while they wait for the set hour, presses on Watson Winwood Reade's popular philosophy treatise.

From the Lyceum the three of them are taken in a four-wheeler through the foggy streets, across the Thames to the

Surrey side and on to the new suburbs that had sprung up round still-expanding London. At last they stop and, admitted to a house by an Indian servant, are greeted by an exceedingly odd individual, Thaddeus Sholto, son of the man who had been Captain Morstan's only friend in London, the former Major Sholto, of the 34th Bombay Infantry. Thaddeus ushers them into his sanctum which he calls 'an oasis of art in the howling desert of South London' and they find themselves looking at tapestries looped back to reveal a richly mounted painting or an Oriental vase, a carpet in amber and black, a lamp 'in the fashion of a silver dove' hanging from an almost invisible golden wire and burning with a subtle and aromatic odour.

We are in the presence of the Aesthetic Movement in its full glory. Thaddeus Sholto is a figure to compare with the movement's unanimously acclaimed high priest, Oscar Wilde – too unanimously perhaps since Wilde was commonly thought to be the target of Gilbert and Sullivan's *Patience*, that great success of 1881, whereas its intended target was the painter-poet Rossetti – though Thaddeus is considerably more effeminate.

Under the Lyceum portico, Miss Mary Morstan's place of rendezvous at the start of *The Sign of Four* affair. A contemporary engraving.

Oscar Wilde: photograph by N. Sarony.

The *Aesthetic Quadrille*, from the *Illustrated London News* of 1882.

But he shares with Wilde two striking facial attributes, a pendulous lip and irregular yellowed teeth (Wilde's teeth had been affected by mercury treatment given for syphilis contracted as an Oxford undergraduate) and both men had a noticeable habit of keeping a hand in front of their mouths. Thaddeus, too, has something of Wilde's gift for outrageous epigram. 'There is nothing', he says in excusing his manner of sending for them, 'more unaesthetic than a policeman.'

It might be expected that Holmes, champion of the Victorian virtues, would have regarded this apparition with contempt. But he does not. When Thaddeus tells them that his father should have divided with Captain Morstan a huge treasure seized in India and that he now proposes to demand Miss Morstan's share, at present in the keeping of his brother, Bartholomew, Holmes says to him directly: 'You have done well, sir, from first to last.'

At Bartholomew's house, Pondicherry Lodge, Norwood, where Holmes gains entrance by recalling to the prize-fighter doorman three rounds they had boxed four years earlier at Alison's Rooms, they find Bartholomew inexplicably murdered in a locked room and the treasure gone. Holmes gets Watson first to accompany Miss Morstan to Mrs Forrester's where, on leaving, he looks back to see, in another of those quietly telling phrases that gleam in his narratives, 'the hall-light shining through stained glass, the barometer, and the bright stair rods', conjuring up in a few words all the solid comfort that said 'Home' to the Victorians. Then Holmes sends Watson to a bird-stuffer's in the lower quarter of Lambeth to hire a dog called Toby, the best beast for tracking in all London.

Soon they are both walking through the dawn streets as Toby eagerly snuffs up the trail of the murderers. 'Labourers and dockmen were already astir, and slatternly women were taking down shutters and brushing doorsteps. At the square-topped corner public-houses business was just beginning, and rough-looking men were emerging, rubbing their sleeves across their beards after their morning wet.' Holmes, looking up at the sun pushing itself over the London cloud-bank, comments on the great elemental forces of Nature and how they ought to make men feel small.

'Are you well up in your Jean Paul?' he asks abruptly.

'Fairly so,' Watson replies. 'I worked back to him through Carlyle.' (Long past teasing now over not knowing who that great man of the age was.)

The Jean Paul whom Holmes spoke of was the German novelist somewhat akin to the Sterne of *A Sentimental Journey*, Jean Paul Richter, who lived between 1763 and 1825 and who now is so little known to English readers that a compendious contemporary reference work like the four-volume *Penguin Companion to Literature* finds no room for him. Yet in Holmes's day he was, as we have seen, so well esteemed that even unbookish Watson had read him. (Will a similar fate overtake our 'Jean-Paul' and Sartre be a name scarcely known a century hence?)

Left: Carlyle.

Right: Jean Paul Richter.

Carlyle, Holmes says, that is like following the brook to the parent lake, and he goes on to quote 'a curious but profound remark' from one of the German's essays: that 'the chief proof of man's real greatness lies in his perception of his own smallness.' It argues, he says, 'a power of comparison and of appreciation which is in itself a proof of nobility. There is much food for thought in Richter. You have not a pistol, have you?'

Watson, this time, has a good heavy stick, and he is more likely as he tramps along behind Toby to be thinking of when he may have to use it than of Richter and Carlyle. Or of the Wilde-like figure they have just met.

Yet were he more given to analysis he might have found the conjunction of these two, Carlyle and Wilde, within the space of one adventurous night in his companion's life of considerable significance. For the two great writers, each so different, represent with almost caricature clarity the two great strains in English intellectual life at this time.

Carlyle, apostle of the old Victorian ideal of Work, tortuous-prosed fount of all that was most Germanic in the then deeply German thought stream of Britain. And Wilde, lucid epigrammatist, the man to whom is often attributed the cheap crack, 'Work is the curse of the drinking classes', writer in French as well as English, representative of the rush to the new. Carlyle, holder up of heroes for his fellow Victorians to worship, exponent of Richter and 'the grandeur of man in his littleness' (the title of the essay which, according to Madeleine B. Stern, learned if perverse author of 'Sherlock Holmes: Rare Book Collector', the detective can have read only in a volume bound up, significantly, with De Quincey's *Confessions of an English Opium Eater*). Wilde, arch-deflator ('To lose one parent, Mr Worthing, may be regarded as a misfortune; to lose both looks like carelessness'), exponent *par excellence*, it may be said, of man's littleness in his grandeur.

Yet Holmes, as we have seen from the approval he gave to the aesthete Thaddeus Sholto, was not squarely on the side of Carlyle and against Wilde. And at the beginning of this adventure we would have found him taking a hypodermic syringe 'from its neat morocco case' and preferring this time cocaine in a seven per cent solution to morphine. 'I abhor the dull routine of existence. I crave for mental exaltation,' he said to Watson. Here is no easy adherent to the great mid-Victorian sense of Order. Nor did he subscribe to the parallel worship of Home. Far from it. He shared with 'Chinese' Gordon all the attitudes of the loner, the outsider. He allowed the presence on his walls of Henry Ward Beecher, at once both upholder of morality and sexual sinner.

There was in Holmes – it was the tragedy he carried within him – an ineradicable something that did not belong to the great Victorian stability which he fought all through his career to preserve. There was in him, as a fixed part of his character, that longing for change, stimulation, excitement which was leading his once solid age, the age of Watson's 'bright stair rods', down a long, long Gadarene slope.

Yet whatever dichotomy lay beneath Holmes's imperturbably hawk-like exterior he was still the hunter, and it did not take him long to bring the mystery of Pondicherry Lodge to a triumphant conclusion. Despite a check or two, before the perpetrators could escape 'to America or the Colonies' he had tracked them down, an ex-convict from the Andaman Islands and his savage monkey-climbing dwarf companion. Only two small blemishes marked the affair. He failed to lay hands on the treasure, which lies now, according to Watson's narrative, somewhere in the Thames mud between Barking Level and Plumstead Marshes. And he lost Watson to Mary Morstan. 'I really cannot congratulate you. . . . Love is an emotional thing, and whatever is emotional is opposed to that true cold reason which I place above all things.' It is how Holmes chose to show himself.

And in the years immediately following there was plenty to

occupy that true cold reason, plenty to provide the mental stimulation Holmes constantly craved, more than a few major engagements in the war which, quarter-crippled within or not, he never flagged in waging. Even before Watson left for married life there was the case he called *The Hound of the Baskervilles*. In it Holmes exhibited some characteristic strokes, immediately perceiving, for instance, the significance of the stolen boot at the Northumberland Hotel (now deservedly renamed the Sherlock Holmes). But it provides us with less information about him than it might since he largely left Watson to conduct operations in the field.

However, near the very start of the affair after Holmes had seen the effect on young Sir Henry Baskerville, fresh from farming in Canada, of the story of the gigantic Dartmoor hound which had perhaps killed his uncle, Sir Charles, we come upon a mere couple of sentences in Watson's story, seemingly no more than a flick of description, which yet tell us a good deal about Sherlock Holmes.

With Watson he had been hurrying along Regent Street shadowing a hansom that was in turn following young Sir Henry

Regent Street, where Holmes and Watson, keeping watch on young Sir Henry Baskerville, were tricked by a mysterious bearded man in a hansom. A contemporary photograph.

Ensor's painting, *Old
Woman with Masks*.

('Your hat and boots, Watson, quick! Not a moment to lose!').
But they are tricked by the bearded man in the cab and lose him.
Then Holmes, with that remarkable power he had of detaching
his mind when there was no grist for it to work on, led Watson
into a picture gallery in near-by Bond Street and for two hours
was 'absorbed in the pictures of the modern Belgian masters'.

Watson says nothing about what painters were on show, only
commenting with a stuffiness that comes right off the page that
Holmes had 'the crudest ideas' about art. But who were the
masters of contemporary Belgian art at that time? They were a
group calling themselves 'the XX', a group led by Félicien Rops
and the half-English James Ensor and including another half-
English artist, the charming but slighter Alfred Stevens. And the

St Mary Magdalene,
by Félicien Rops.

theory to which they gave their allegiance was none other than
the Symbolism of the French literary *avant-garde*, at that time
happy to number among its adherents Oscar Wilde, author in
French of that richly decorative play, *Salomé*.

Of Ensor's work Holmes might have seen in 1888 his *Carnival
on the Beach*, a painting typical of the artist's love of masks and the
mysterious, swept like most of his pictures by a pallid light with
here and there glittering flashes of yellow and vermilion,
exaggerated and caricature-like. Or he might have seen the
drawing *The Devil Leading Christ into Hell*. Had the exhibition
been a year or so later it could have contained a work which
shocked even Ensor's fellow iconoclasts of the XX Group when
only his own vote saved him from expulsion, the *Entry of Christ
into Brussels* with its banner 'Vive la Sociale' and its message that
on arriving Jesus would be treated just as in Jerusalem.

Of the work of Rops, friend of Baudelaire, poet of *Les Fleurs du
Mal*, much admired by other French writers (no one, said the
Goncourt brothers, had better expressed 'The cruel aspect of
contemporary woman, her steely glance, her malevolence
towards men'), Holmes could have seen the etchings called *Les
Sataniques* or the paintings *Les Monstres* and *La Buveuse d'Absinthe*.

Watson, stolid British Watson, standing beside him, could
hardly have approved. So his condemnation of Holmes's views
on art as crude can mean only that Holmes expressed admiration

for such work, revealing yet again, subjected to the vision of the
artists, that buried part of himself which lay in such pole-like
opposition to the ideas and beliefs for which he was even at that
instant fighting.

The ideas of the supremacy of the rational and of the scientific
method, however, were perhaps never more to the fore than in
Holmes's conduct of this case apparently so redolent of hours
when, to quote the Baskerville manuscript, 'the powers of evil are
exalted'. From the first Holmes saw that if Sir Henry's boots had
been stolen from the Northumberland Hotel, then it was no
supernatural hound that was prowling Dartmoor by night. And
at the end he was able indeed to fish from the bog mud the very
piece of footwear used to set the flesh-and-blood beast on Sir
Henry's trail.

But there was an evil abroad in the case that was fully
consonant with the scientific ideas of Holmes's age. This was the

Holmes rescues from the Dartmoor mire Sir Henry Baskerville's missing boot. Paget's illustration.

ever-lurking and feared danger of the atavistic, of the man walking among his sensible nineteenth-century fellows who was a throwback for purely scientific reasons to some deeper and darker age. For an era that had plunged on the notion of progress, of the great world speeding ahead along the ringing grooves of change, an era when the general belief was, in the

Jekyll turns into Hyde. Illustration by S.G. Hulme-Beaman to R.L. Stevenson's immensely popular story.

Photograph of Alphonse Bertillon, using his own methods of anthropological measurement.

words of Holmes's favourite Winwood Reade, 'that the genius of man has been developed along a line of unbroken descent from the simple tendencies which inhabited the primitive cell' and that 'a glorious futurity' lay ahead, how appalling it must have been to have to contemplate the possibility that a great leap backwards could take place. No wonder Robert Louis Stevenson's account of the terrible Mr Hyde buried in the benevolent Dr Jekyll so gripped the imagination of Holmes's contemporaries.

In the Baskerville case this thought was always very much in the air. The country doctor who first interested Holmes in the business proved to be an anthropologist of some standing, a prize essayist with 'Is Disease A Reversion?' and author of a *Lancet* article, 'Some Freaks of Atavism'. He greeted Holmes, too, with 'I had hardly expected so dolichocephalic a skull or such well-marked supra-orbital development' and was soon comparing him, slightly to his disadvantage (Holmes was piqued), to the great contemporary French criminal anthropologist, Bertillon. And when on the Moor they glimpsed an escaped convict it was a terrible animal face they saw, 'all seamed and scored with vile passions', a face that might have belonged to 'one of those old

A face that might have belonged to an ancient savage. Paget's portrayal of the escaped Dartmoor convict.

savages who dwelt in the burrows on the hillsides'. Finally, in exposing the local mild naturalist as the villain, Holmes observed, his eyes 'trained to examine faces and not their trimmings', a portrait of the wicked Sir Hugo Baskerville of old that fundamentally resembled that apparent stranger and so discovered that there was the final heir to the Baskerville estates, 'a throwback' to the evil roisterer.

The atavistic comes up explicitly again in Watson's account of the Greek Interpreter, where incidentally one of the criminals turns out to be 'a man of the foulest antecedents'. After tea one summer evening, Watson tells us, 'the conversation, which had roamed in a desultory, spasmodic fashion from golf clubs to the causes of the change in the obliquity of the ecliptic' – this from Holmes, the man who knew nothing of the solar system – 'came round at last to the question of atavism and hereditary aptitudes.' Watson suggested then that Holmes's 'faculty of observation and your peculiar facility for deduction are due to your own systematic training.'

Princetown Prison, Dartmoor, from which a convict with a face 'all scarred and scored with vile passions' escaped to add to the complications of the Baskerville affair. An early 1890s photograph.

Claude Joseph
Vernet's painting *A
Storm with a Shipwreck*,
fruit of his
experimentalist
shipboard ordeal,
lashed to the mast
during a tempest.

'To some extent,' Holmes answered thoughtfully. 'My
ancestors were country squires, who appear to have led much the
same life as is natural to their class' – oh, spirit of Victorian
stability! – 'but, none the less, my turn that way is in my veins,
and may have come with my grandmother, who was the sister of
Vernet, the French artist. Art in the blood is liable to take the
strangest forms.'

'Vernet, the French artist' poses somewhat of a problem: there
were dozens of artist Vernets. The first, according to an article by
Ben Wolf in the *Baker Street Journal*, was Antoine Vernet
(1689–1753), father of twenty-two children. Four of these were
recognized painters, of whom Claude Joseph Vernet
(1714–1789) had himself, in the best experimentalist tradition,
lashed to a ship's mast during a storm to observe the effects. He
painted in the highly romantic manner of Salvator Rosa, one of
whose works Holmes saw in the lush Aesthetic study of Thaddeus
Sholto. Claude Joseph Vernet had a son, Antoine Charles
Horace, known as Carle Vernet (1758–1836), whose *Morning of
Austerlitz* gained him the Légion d'Honneur (Holmes won his in
1894 for tracking Huret, the Boulevard assassin, Watson tells us),
and Carle in turn had a son, Horace Vernet (1789–1863). The
dates would indicate then that Holmes's grandmother ought to
be this last's sister, Carle Vernet's daughter. Mendelssohn,

Left: Carle Vernet, Holmes's presumptive great-grandfather.

Below: Lithograph after Horace Vernet's painting of his own studio, with its boxers and fencers.

Queen Victoria's favourite composer, records of Horace Vernet that he had a mind so orderly that it was like a well-stocked bureau in which he had but to open a drawer to find what he needed ('I hold a vast store of out-of-the-way knowledge, without scientific system, but very available for the needs of my work,' Holmes was to say of himself in his account of the Lion's Mane case) and so keen was the painter's observation that a single glance at a model was enough to let him record the minutest details. Horace Vernet painted himself in his studio once with two models fencing and another wearing boxing-gloves. So he, too, must have loved the sports at which Holmes excelled.

But hardly had Watson had this unique glimpse of his friend's ancestry than Holmes added something yet more astonishing. How did he know his singular gift was hereditary, Watson had asked.

'Because my brother Mycroft possesses it in a larger degree than I do.'

And so we learn of the existence of a second Holmes. But he is a Holmes deficient, we are told, in ambition and energy, 'absolutely incapable of working out the practical points which

Mycroft Holmes, as visualized by Sidney Paget.

must be gone into before a case could be laid before a judge or jury.' He is in Government service, Sherlock says, and later, when at the time of the Bruce-Partington case he knows Watson yet better, he confides in him that 'you would be right in a sense if you said that occasionally he *is* the British Government', even though he draws no more than £450 a year, since with 'the greatest capacity for storing facts of any man living' he alone can swiftly co-ordinate the most diverse of fields and seize on a correct policy.

At about this time Holmes began to detect from his many sources in the underworld of London the presence of some organizing figure behind the worst crimes of the day. He knew who this was – a much more dangerous example of the atavistic than any he has yet encountered, one Professor James Moriarty, in Holmes's own words 'a man of good birth and excellent education, endowed by Nature with a phenomenal mathematical faculty. . . . But the man had hereditary tendencies of the most diabolical kind. A criminal strain ran in his blood.' Holmes

Clubland Pall Mall, where, the establishment Watson calls the Diogenes, Mycroft Holmes's habitual lair, was to be found. An 1895 photograph.

George Meredith.

had already clashed with him indirectly once, in the *Valley of Fear* case when the man whose life he had saved from the American Scowrers was eventually hunted down by Moriarty.

Now at the beginning of the 1890s the Professor was increasingly engaging Holmes's attention. But there were to be a good many other cases before any final confrontation between the two. There was the occasion when Holmes obliged the Pope in the matter of the Vatican Cameos. There was the Herefordshire murder in the Boscombe Valley, in the course of which we hear of Holmes reading both Petrarch, that fourteenth-century Italian sonneteer of a love that could never be consummated, and Meredith, novelist of his own day, toilsome now to get through but full of a wit much like Holmes's own, a writer who ever refused to lower his standards for commercial success, friend also of Rossetti and of Swinburne, sensuous singer of the perverse.

There was, too, at this period, among cases too numerous even to name, the affair of the Tired Captain and Holmes's intervention in the matter of the Naval Treaty, 'an interference which had the unquestionable effect of preventing a serious international complication', not for the first time. There was as well the case of the Crooked Man ('Excellent,' Watson cried: 'Elementary,' said Holmes). And there was the Silver Blaze case,

Professor Moriarty:
portrait by Sidney Paget.

when Holmes travelled down to the Dartmoor training stables at King's Pyland to display at its fullest his extraordinary power of seeing the essential in any matter. ('Is there any other point to which you would wish to draw my attention?' 'To the curious incident of the dog in the night-time.' 'The dog did nothing in the night-time.' 'That was the curious incident.') Finally there was the 'three-pipe problem' of the Red-headed League in which Holmes at last frustrated the cunning plot whereby that effeminate grandson of a Royal Duke, the ex-Etonian John Clay, 'murderer, thief, smasher, and forger' in the words of Inspector Athelney Jones, hoped to steal a fortune through persuading the vain and pompous pawnbroker Jabez Wilson that he could earn easy money by copying out the *Encyclopaedia Britannica* since as a really red-headed man he could benefit under a curious will.

Clay and his associates safely under lock and key ('If they fire, Watson, have no compunction about shooting them down'),

Holmes with Silver Blaze.

Holmes lays hands on John Clay,
'murderer, thief, smasher and forger'.

Holmes with that show of modesty that is really the proud man's
sharpest boast commented: the man is nothing, the work
everything. '"L'homme c'est rien – l'oeuvre c'est tout" as
Gustave Flaubert wrote to Georges Sand.' (Watson, typically,
gets the French a little wrong; the first 'c'est' should be 'n'est' and
there is no second 'c'est' nor did the pseudonymous lady novelist
spell her George in the French manner.)

But the quotation is significant. The volume of letters in which
it is to be found had been published only a few years earlier. We
see Holmes then as especially well up in contemporary French
intellectual life. But more. His interest in these two authors sheds
an extra light on him. Flaubert had long been a figure of
notoriety, put on trial for offences against public morals after the
publication of *Madame Bovary*, the great exponent of art for art's
sake, of everything indeed for art's sake, author of the exotic and
savage *Salammbô*, excoriator of all bourgeois conventionalism
(Watson liked the 'fine sea stories' of Clark Russell, the
Hammond Innes of his day). George Sand, famed for her

Flaubert.

trousers and her lovers who included Chopin, Liszt and Alfred de Musset, condemned by Carlyle, our chief upholder of the Victorian virtues of old, for 'a new and astonishing Phallus-Worship, with universal Balzac-Sand melodies and litanies' and by Thackeray, who called her novel *Lélia* 'a regular topsyturvyfication of morality, a thieves' and prostitutes' apotheosis.' Here is yet one more shaft of light down into the hidden part of Holmes.

Yet he was fighting still for those old virtues, and now against his greatest enemy, still only to be dimly perceived in the shadows, Professor Moriarty, that man with hereditary tendencies of the most diabolical kind. It was to be a battle on even terms.

'The famous scientific criminal, as famous among crooks as –'

'My blushes, Watson,' Holmes murmured.

'I was about to say "as he is unknown to the public".'

'A touch – a distinct touch!' cried Holmes. 'You are developing a certain unexpected strain of pawky humour, Watson.'

What else do we know from Watson's narratives of this Napoleon of crime, with his face 'for ever oscillating from side to side in a curiously reptilian fashion'? We know that he had two brothers, one a colonel, the other a station-master. He was the author, at the age of twenty-one, of a treatise on the binomial

George Sand.

theorem that gained him a European vogue and his university chair, and his book *The Dynamics of An Asteroid* (Einstein in 1905 was to write *The Electrodynamics of Moving Bodies*) ascended to such rarefied heights that there was no man in the scientific Press capable of reviewing it. We know that when he was forced to leave his university because dark rumours were circulating he became, as a cover for his criminal activities, an Army coach (these were the great early days of entry to the State professions by competitive examination, a mark of the burgeoning technocratic age) and that he was an excellent instructor, enlightening Inspector MacDonald wonderfully on eclipses when that excellent fellow with his 'good Aberdeen upbringing' went, after Holmes's hints, to take a cautious look at him.

Nietzsche, extoller of the Superman.

But we can add something to the facts of Watson's accounts. Because Moriarty bears a telling likeness to another man of the period who gained a university chair in his twenties and subsequently had to resign it, another 'genius, philosopher, abstract thinker' – the words are Holmes's own labels for Moriarty – who became execrated as a figure of evil: the German Friedrich Nietzsche.

Nietzsche, philosopher, abstract thinker and a recognized genius, was not unknown in England at least to those acquainted with German culture at this time, and the influence of Germany then was enormously much stronger than it has been at any period since the start of the First World War, ranging from the championship of Carlyle, down through the ineradicable

At the London
Militärverein,
drinking the health of
the Kaiser. A
photograph from
about 1900.

German accent of Edward, Prince of Wales, to the 'German
Ocean', now the North Sea – Holmes looks sombrely at its 'violet
rim' at a low point in his tackling of the Dancing Men case – to
London clubs like the Militär Verein and newspapers like the
Londoner Zeitung, right down to the presence in the streets
everywhere of German bands and in hotels of what the
contemporary historian T.H.S. Escott called 'the ubiquitous
German waiters', one of whom Holmes questioned during the
Baskerville case.

Nietzsche was the man who had dared to criticize, and with
passion, both Christianity ('God is dead') and bourgeois
conformism. He was seen for long, however he may be thought of
now, as yet another manifestation of the rot that had set in with

Darwin's overturning of the time-sealed order of things. In place of the picture of man's mind as a rational machine current, if not unchallenged, since the days of Locke in the seventeenth century he proposed a panorama of darkness and treacherous hidden depths. His book *The Birth of Tragedy*, in those days his most influential work, had drawn a vivid contrast between the orderliness that belonged to Apollo, the bright sun god, and the deliberately sought wildness of the disciples of Dionysus, god of fertility, otherwise Bacchus. And he insisted that Dionysus must be given his due, that through music, rhythm and dance (and by implication drugs, like a seven per cent solution of cocaine) man must achieve heightened states of being. He put forward the idea of the Superman and that human weakness, 'all too human weaknesses', was bringing a crisis of self-hatred to European civilization, a twilight of the gods, an idea echoed by his admired friend Richard Wagner.

At the end of the Red Circle affair Holmes was to drag Watson to a Covent Garden Wagner night: 'if we hurry, we might be in time for the second act.' So we may well ask if Holmes, the superman detective, did not share with his equal and opposite opponent, Moriarty, more than a little of the Nietzschean attitudes.

A twilight of the gods, a coming to an end. The nineteenth century was coming to an end, and sensitive and intellectual men everywhere felt it, Sherlock Holmes clearly among them. '*Fin de siècle*' became the general cry, a label that was soon slapped on anything that remotely had the characteristics of hectic novelty-seeking in the face of a new unknown, slapped on (to quote Holbrook Jackson, who not only actively lived through the period but extensively chronicled it) to 'anything strange or uncommon, anything which savoured of freak and perversity'. Those years were a rich orchid-flowering of all that there had been in the Aesthetic Movement that preceded them. And Holmes who, as we have seen, already had in him much from that period, much in opposition to the stable times in which he had grown up, did not fail to respond in his turn.

'My mind rebels at stagnation,' he said to Watson in defending his use of drugs. 'Crime is commonplace,' he shouted in exasperation. 'Existence is commonplace.' He believed in art for art's sake. 'To the man who loves art for its own sake,' he said at the beginning of the adventure of the Copper Beeches, tossing aside *The Daily Telegraph*, 'it is frequently in its least important and lowliest manifestations that the keenest pleasure is to be derived,' and when the freakish circumstances of the

Opposite: Wagner's *Siegfried* at Covent Garden in 1892. An *Illustrated London News* engraving.

Stockbroker's Clerk case were put before him he had, Watson tells us, a look on his face 'like a connoisseur who had just taken his first sip of a comet vintage'. Finding a few idle words during the Naval Treaty business to cover up his examination of the window of the room where he suspects the missing document is hidden, he pulls in a rose and reflects, 'this rose is an extra. Its smell and its colour are an embellishment of life, not a condition of it. It is only goodness which gives extras, and so I say again that we have much to hope from the flowers.' This is very near to the saying of Ruskin's that lies at the heart of art-for-art's-sake, of the high elevation of beauty for itself. 'The flower is the end or proper object of the seed.'

But Holmes had in him as well as this the push-onward of that philosophy that had brought about the worship of 'anything that savoured of freak'. A favourite word of his was *'outré'* and he says teasingly to Watson of the Stockbroker's Clerk affair that it 'at least presents those unusual and *outré* features which are as dear to you as they are to me.' Even Inspector Lestrade, least observant of the Scotland Yarders, noticed this about Holmes. Seeking his aid, in as roundabout a way as he could manage, in the case of the Six Napoleons, he said, 'on the other hand, although it is trivial, it is undoubtedly queer, and I know that you have a taste for all that is out of the common.' And through Watson's pages this taste of Holmes's became known even to prospective clients, like the retired colourman who, begging Watson to secure Holmes's help, said, 'of course, it is art for art's sake with him.'

There is, too, another trait well developed in Holmes which was a keynote of the *fin de siècle* movement, the desire to shock. Wilde, the strong link between the aesthetes of the eighties and the rarer hot-house blooms of the nineties, as he is our greatest contrast with the sterner earlier age of Carlyle, possessed this quality above all. And above all he showed it in his novel published at the beginning of this decade, one of its testaments, *The Picture of Dorian Gray*.

> 'If we women did not love you for your defects, where would you all be? Not one of you would ever be married. You would be a set of unfortunate bachelors. Not, however, that that would alter you much. Nowadays all the married men live like bachelors and all the bachelors like married men!'
> *'Fin de siècle,'* murmured Sir Henry.
> *'Fin du globe,'* answered his hostess.
> 'I wish it were *fin du globe*,' said Dorian, with a sigh. 'Life is a great disappointment.'

'This rose is an extra': Sherlock
Holmes in uncharacteristically lyrical
mood in the Naval Treaty case.

The extract says a lot. Even to a new attitude to bachelors. In
the sterner days bachelors had been looked on as beings of a
superior order. Magazine-writers had drawn up lists of famous
bachelors from Newton to Beethoven, including even Jesus
Christ, and they might well have added the name of Sherlock
Holmes. Now bachelors are derided. And note another thing:
bachelor Holmes is well capable of keeping up his end with
young Dorian or the world-weary Sir Henry in the epigram
game. 'Depend upon it there is nothing so unnatural as the
commonplace' ('A Case of Identity'), 'I read nothing except the
criminal news and the agony column. The latter is always
instructive' ('The Noble Bachelor'), 'I never make exceptions.
An exception disproves the rule' (*The Sign of Four*).

Yet there was in the *fin-de-siècle* efflorescence something that
was still repellent to the Holmes we know, besides those outward
signs which he both disapproved of and half-welcomed. It is
an aggressiveness. Holbrook Jackson put it well. A chief

characteristic of the period was, he says, 'a demand for wider ranges, newer emotional and spiritual territories, fresh woods and pastures new for the soul. If you will, it is a form of imperialism of the spirit, ambitious, arrogant, aggressive, waving the flag of human power over an ever wider and wider territory.' Its hecticness is 'the unrest of an age grown too big for its boots'. Behind the clamorous calls of the poet Dowson 'for madder music and for stronger wine' we see the shadow of that altogether unWildean figure, the noisy royal Tum-Tum, one day to be Emperor of India.

The aggressive, imperialistic note came to sound more and more loudly everywhere as the nineties grew to their height. So it should come as no surprise to detect in Holmes at this point the first signs of a weariness, of a desire to lay down the weapons he has fought with so long and so well. 'I think I may go so far as to say, Watson, that I have not lived wholly in vain. If my record were closed to-night I could still survey it with equanimity. The air of London is the sweeter for my presence.' Contrast this with Watson's own description of London at the beginning of their alliance as 'that great cesspool into which all the loungers and idlers of the Empire are irresistibly drained'.

But there was one great opponent to meet and match before any real thought of laying down arms could be considered, the genius, philosopher and abstract thinker of crime, Professor Moriarty.

It was on the 24th of April 1891 that Holmes walked one evening into the consulting-room at Watson's abode of married bliss, edged his way round the walls, flung the shutters together over the window, bolted them securely and, dropping into a chair, showed his old friend the burst and bleeding knuckles of his right hand.

He then recounted to Watson the way in which his long, secret battle with Moriarty had at last brought the man himself to Baker Street. 'You crossed my path on the 4th of January,' Moriarty had said. 'On the 23rd you incommoded me; by the middle of February I was seriously inconvenienced by you; at the end of March I was absolutely hampered in my plans.' Holmes, naturally, had declined to draw back. 'If you are clever enough', Moriarty had said, 'to bring destruction upon me, rest assured that I shall do as much to you.'

'You have paid me several compliments, Mr Moriarty,' Holmes had answered. 'Let me pay you one in return when I say that if I were assured of the former eventuality I would, in the interests of the public, cheerfully accept the latter.'

Holmes disguised as a
venerable Italian priest,
evading Moriarty.

Holmes told Watson then that he needed to avoid for a few days more the murderous attacks of Moriarty's henchmen such as the 'gentleman upon whose front teeth I have barked my knuckles' and then his trap could be sprung. Watson agreed to accompany his friend to the Continent for that period, finding him next morning in a first-class compartment of the Dover express disguised as a venerable Italian priest. And, even though Moriarty engaged a special and followed them racketing along the rails, they succeeded in getting safely to France and making their way, not without a sign or two that they were still pursued, to Switzerland.

But there, as they arrived at the tremendous and awe-inspiring Falls at Reichenbach, a Swiss lad came running after them with a note from the hotel at Meiringen where they had spent the night asking Watson to return and give his professional services to an English lady dying of consumption. 'The appeal was one which could not be ignored', Watson tells us, and so he

Holmes gazes at the
Reichenbach Falls.

hurried away, casting one last glance back at his friend gazing down at the rush of the mighty waters.

But at the hotel the note proved a forgery. Watson raced back, to find only a letter from Holmes.

My dear Watson, I write these few lines by the courtesy of Mr Moriarty, who awaits my convenience for the final discussion of those questions which lie between us. . . . I have already explained to you . . . that my career had in any case reached its crisis. . . . Indeed, if I may make a full confession to you, I was quite convinced that the letter from Meiringen was a hoax. . . . Pray give my greetings to Mrs Watson, and believe me to be, my dear fellow,

Very sincerely yours,

SHERLOCK HOLMES

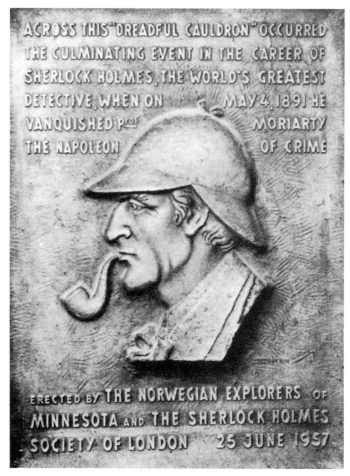

Plaque at the Reichenbach Falls.

Park Lane about
1896. It was
hereabouts that
Watson made his
forlorn examination
of the scene of the
murder of the Hon
Ronald Adair.

However Sherlock Holmes, English gentleman, was not dead.
But it was to be nearly three long years before Watson saw him
again and our record of his life can resume. One day in the spring
of 1894 while Watson was in Park Lane glumly inspecting the
site of the murder in a locked room of the Hon. Ronald Adair, in
the delusive hope of being able to apply the methods of his late
and much lamented friend, he accidentally knocked into an
elderly deformed man and tipped some books he was carrying to
the ground – *The Origins of Tree Worship* was a title that caught
his eye – but when he had attempted to apologize the hunchback
had turned away with a snarl. Back at home, Watson was
surprised to be called on by the cripple who offered to sell him
British Birds, *The Holy War* and a volume of Catullus. 'You could
just fill that gap on that second shelf.'

Watson looks at the gap, turns back and there standing
smiling at him across his study table, disguise thrown off in an
instant, is Sherlock Holmes. Watson 'for the first and last time in
my life' faints clean away.

Revived with brandy, he heard from Holmes how he had not, as it had seemed, plunged to death with the Napoleonic, Nietzschean Professor Moriarty. But he had found, when the Professor's body had tumbled into the fearful chasm, that he himself was still being pursued, by a certain Colonel Sebastian Moran, Indian Army retired, Moriarty's lieutenant and the second most dangerous man in London. So for three years he had kept out of the way, biding his time. He had travelled in Tibet, visiting like many another intrepidly self-confident Victorian explorer the unvisitable, spending some days with the Head Lama in Lhasa; in Arabia he had gone in disguise to prohibited

Watson accidentally knocks into an elderly deformed bookseller beneath the window where Ronald Adair met his mysterious death.

Sir Richard Burton, explorer, in disguise.

Mecca like another loner eccentric of the time, Sir Richard Burton, first translator of the unexpurgated *Thousand and One Nights*; he had met at Khartoum the Khalifa, successor to the Mahdi whose men had slain Gordon. Then he had come nearer, to France, where in Montpellier he had researched into the coal-tar derivatives, those prolific substances which had among other things given the ladies of the time the garish colours their triumphant menfolk so delighted to see them in.

And Watson? What of him in this interim? He had been bereaved. The former Miss Mary Morstan had died (we are never told how) and so he was free now to sell his practice and join Holmes again in the old rooms at Baker Street, faithfully preserved by Mrs Hudson, soon to be joined in her attendance by Billy, the page-boy. A young Dr Verner gave Watson the highest price he had ventured to ask for his practice, and only years later did the good doctor discover he had sold to a distant relative of Holmes's who was paying with Holmes's money.

And what about those books which a hunted Holmes – Moriarty's men were sworn to revenge – had taken about with him? *British Birds* can pass without comment as simply good disguise. But *The Origins of Tree Worship*? That surely tells us that Holmes the anthropologist follower of Darwin is still as he was. And *The Holy War*? Surely an affirmation that the struggle to

preserve the ordered, home-loving, Bunyan-on-Sundays society of his young days will still be pursued. But Catullus? Catullus, the Roman poet who described a love a good deal more complex ('*Odi et amo*,' he wrote. 'I love and I hate together') than Watson's stolid domestic bliss? Catullus, who did not hesitate to use the Latin four-letter word *futo* and others in the most explicit manner? Yet here is Holmes clutching a volume of his verses. In his three-year absence the other, dark, hidden part of him clearly had not withered away.

But now he is menaced directly by Colonel Moran, the self-same man who had been playing cards with the Hon. Ronald Adair on the night he died and who, in Holmes's words, 'undoubtedly played foul'. We are back to Tranby Croft as well as 'the atrocious conduct of Colonel Upwood in connection with the famous card scandal of the Nonpareil Club' mentioned in *The Hound of the Baskervilles*. Moran's career had been that of 'an honourable soldier', the best shot in India. But, Holmes says, 'there are some trees, Watson, which grow to a certain height and then suddenly develop some unsightly eccentricity. You will see it often in humans. I have a theory that the individual represents in his development the whole procession of his ancestors, and that such a sudden turn to good or evil stands for some strong influence which came into the line of his pedigree.'

A French workshop for the manufacture of aniline dyes. It was at Montpellier that Holmes, during his time in hiding, researched into the coal-tar derivatives, of which aniline is one.

It is the atavistic again, the threat lurking for all progress-trusting Victorians.

To outwit Moran, Holmes takes Watson now by a twisting route through the London by-ways he knows so well into an empty house. Peering through its window Watson sees they are exactly opposite the old rooms at 221B Baker Street and in the window across the street there, to his astonishment, is none other than Sherlock Holmes, the well-loved profile lamp-lit. It is a bust, Holmes explains, made by Oscar Meunier, of Grenoble. At quarter-hourly intervals poor Mrs Hudson creeps along and shifts it a little. ('Of course it has moved. Am I such a farcical bungler, Watson, that I should erect an obvious dummy?') Before long the decoy for Colonel Moran fulfils its task, and London is rid of an evil man and Sherlock Holmes can openly take up his profession again.

Years in general very busy followed, though they were not without their fallow weeks when nothing of interest presented itself to the great detective and Watson would dread that the

Colonel Moran, 'the second most dangerous man in London', is captured in the empty house opposite 221B Baker Street.

drug mania from which he hoped he had gradually weaned his friend would return, 'for I was well aware that the fiend was not dead, but sleeping.'

There was at this time the business of ex-President Murillo in which violent Latin America once more reached out to send a tremor through still relatively stable old England. There was the shocking affair of the Dutch steamer *Friesland*, which nearly cost both Holmes and Watson their lives. There was the sudden death of Cardinal Tosca and the arrest of Wilson, the notorious canary-trainer. There was the matter of the Three Students and cheating in the examinations (what a falling away from the standards of the gentleman). There was the Black Peter case and that of the Norwood Builder, which gave Watson no cause to whisper a warning 'Norbury' in Holmes's ear despite Inspector Lestrade admitting, 'this is the brightest thing you have done yet.' There were the businesses of the Veiled Lodger, of the Sussex Vampire, of the Missing Three-quarter and of the equally missing Bruce-Partington plans, already referred to. So it was not to be wondered at that by the spring of 1897 Holmes was once more on the verge of a breakdown (or that particularly Victorian malady, brain-fever, suffered by so many of the people he encountered in his cases). But, sent on the orders of Dr Moore Agar, of Harley Street, to recuperate in Cornwall, Holmes still dealt briskly with the Devil's Foot affair in which, experimenting with an unknown substance from Africa, he unwittingly imperilled Watson's life and showed him in the aftermath more of his heart than he had ever done before.

The world to which Sherlock Holmes had returned from the dead was as hard to defend as ever, or harder. Perhaps a check in the long slide-away from the solid virtues of old had come in 1895 when Oscar Wilde, counter-standard-bearer to earnest old Carlyle, had been disgraced in two sensational trials, had had his books withdrawn by his publishers and his plays taken off in the theatres. 'The crash of the fall certainly affected the whole spirit of this year,' wrote R. H. Gretton in his almost contemporary *Modern History of the English People*. 'There were few great houses in London where he was not known; fewer still where there was not among the younger generation an aggressive, irresponsible intolerance which had some relation, however vague, to his brilliant figure. Even athleticism rejoiced at this date to disassociate itself from anything that might have been in danger of easy approval from an older generation, by being too aesthetic; captains of university football teams had been seen with long hair.'

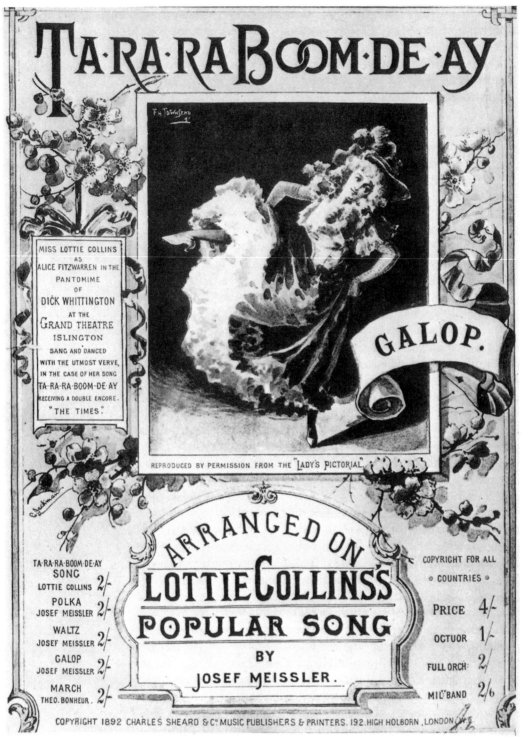

'Ta-ra-ra Boom-de-ay': sheet music, 1892.

But the check, if check there was, was short-lived. Certainly there was everywhere an increasing note of raucousness as the century approached its end. While Holmes had been in Tibet a song very different from 'Home, Sweet Home' had swept the country. In 1892 Lottie Collins had given her public 'Ta-ra-ra Boom-de-ay' and for at least the next four years that bouncily vulgar tune was to be heard in all of London's fifty music-halls and pretty well everywhere else. There was an increasing grandiloquence, too, with new huge and uncompromisingly ugly public buildings rising up in London and in every other major city. And as the century reached its very end the figures for book publication came out: novels, 1,825; religion, 590. (In the Golden Pince-nez case at Yoxley Old Court in the year of Holmes's return he outplayed old Professor Coram whose boast it was that his work on the Coptic monasteries would 'cut deep at the very foundation of revealed religion.')

Another indication of the way things were going can be seen in a case Watson felt had points 'which made it stand out in those long records of crime from which I gather the material for these little narratives.' It is the affair of the Solitary Cyclist, on the face of it quite a minor matter in which Holmes's assistance had been begged by the governess, or more specifically music teacher, Miss Violet Smith. Holmes, Watson tells us, took her hand. 'I nearly fell into the error of supposing that you were typewriting. Of course, it is obvious that it is music. You observe that spatulate finger-end, Watson, which is common to both professions? There is a spirituality about the face, however, which the typewriter does not generate.' The age, we see, is moving on: there is another course than the hardships of a governess's life open to the impoverished lady, though it is one that bestows an independence which carries dangers of its own, as Holmes had already seen with a typewriting lady on the fringes of the Baskerville case.

Danger and independence are linked again in this affair. Violet Smith is so keen a bicycle-rider that, but for Holmes's last-minute intervention, she would have suffered, in Watson's words, 'the worst fate that can befall a woman', even if in her case it had had a sort of legality conferred on it by a mock wedding performed by a rogue clergyman.

The bicycle, after not a few trials and errors – the celerifere, the velocifere, the draisienne, the Gompertz velocipede, the aellopede, the penny-farthing, the dicycle, the tricycle, the quadricycle (one of which was ridden by our friend Thomas Carlyle as early as 1849) – had come to reasonable perfection with the invention of Dunlop's pneumatic tyre in 1888. From then on it had had its considerable social effects. Up till then the world, it is not going too far to say, had been divided into walkers and horse-owners; now there was an intermediate class. The advent of the cycle meant even for the horsed a lessening of all the complications of stables and grooms. It put, too, within the range of many common folk all sorts of goods that had before been almost unobtainable. Flora Thompson, author of *Lark Rise to Candleford*, recalls how just before this time it was necessary for a village-dweller to tramp six or seven miles if she wanted a reel of thread. Cycling ended another complication as well: it meant that the chaperon had more and more to be abandoned (as Violet Smith nearly learnt to her cost). But the two wheels also brought happiness. They gave to many individuals who would never otherwise have known it the whole of the countryside. They were, in Holbrook Jackson's words, 'the instrument of a new freedom'.

'You observe that spatulate finger-end, Watson?' From the spirituality about Miss Violet Smith's face Holmes chooses music and not the typewriter as cause of the peculiarity. A Paget illustration from Watson's account of the 'Solitary Cyclist' case.

Miss Violet Smith, the solitary cyclist, pursued. Paget's view of an incident in the affair.

One more mark of Britain's increasingly rapid descent from the dignified calm of yore may be seen in another of Holmes's cases from this period, the affair of the Dancing Men. For its unfortunate victim, Mr Hilton Cubitt, of Ridling Thorpe Manor, Norfolk, its terrible events began with an occasion that was meant to be all sun, Queen Victoria's Diamond Jubilee of 1897, when, coming up to London for the celebrations, he met a young American lady, Miss Elsie Patrick.

But what celebrations they were. The day of jubilee exceeded in every dimension the Golden Jubilee of ten years before, perhaps because the monarch who had said 'everyone comments on *my* simplicity' was now often in a wheel-chair, her formidable energies worn down by age and sorrows. So her subjects were able, uninhibited, to splurge on congratulating themselves on a Great White Queen upon whose Empire 'the sun never set', a phrase coined indeed in 1897 and now done to death. This was the climax of the process which had begun in that significant

time a quarter of a century earlier with Disraeli's firm turn to Imperialism in his Crystal Palace speech of 1872. Victoria, her propagandists boasted now, ruled over more human beings, speaking more languages and practising more religions than had any sovereign before in the whole history of the world.

So Empire was rampant, and the Jubilee was, in the words of the historian David Thomson, a 'gigantic advertisement' for the Imperial achievement. Indeed, this was altogether an era of advertisement. As the years had gone by the blaring clamour of commerce had grown louder and louder. Turn the pages of any long-running periodical of the time such as the *Illustrated London News* and you can see it happening. Year by year more and more space is devoted to advertisements. Year by year they get larger. Year by year their type gets blacker. Eventually even that celebrated detective, Mr Sherlock Holmes, is pressed, unasked, into service to extol the virtues of Beecham's Pills, while of a parallel field the paper's resident essayist, James Payn, wrote: 'Everyone knows that one way of getting preferment is to advertise beforehand that you have got it. . . . Scarcely anyone succeeds to the judicial ermine or to lawn sleeves without sending up a balloon of this kind.' (As early as 1881 Sherlock Holmes had

The last Letter from SHERLOCK HOLMES.

——— ◆◆◆◆◆ ———

"Dear Friend,—Mystery follows mystery; but the most mysterious thing of all is what has become of the part of my system which has almost taken the form of my second nature. I was especially cautious to provide myself with the indispensable before leaving home, but it has disappeared and I have lost all trace. I have unravelled many of other people's losses, but here is one of my own which has thrown me on my beam ends. I would not have troubled you, but in this benighted spot—although you will scarcely credit it—I cannot procure what I much need; so send by <u>first</u> post, as my movements are uncertain, one large box of Beecham's Pills. Note my assumed name and enclosed address, which I beg of you to destroy, as I do not wish my whereabouts to be known.   "Yours,   S. H."

said bitterly at the conclusion of the *Study in Scarlet* case: 'What you do in this world is a matter of no consequence. The question is, what can you make people believe that you have done?')

But elsewhere the *Illustrated London News* sounded a less cynical note. Come the great day, its tame poet, Cosmo Monkhouse, sang out proprietorially:

> *Wherever sounds the wave or blows the wind,*
> *Thy name is sounded and thy fame is blown,*
> *Queen of the Seas, and Empress of the Ind,*
> *Great and our own.*

And to a pageant whose splendour a *Daily Mail* writer claimed 'has never been parallelled in the history of the world' (even the ranks of France could scarce forbear to cheer: 'Rome has been equalled if not surpassed,' said *Le Figaro*) there came not only all the crowned heads of Europe but eleven Premiers of British colonies together with representatives of every aspect of the land-eating Empire, rajahs and maharajahs from 'our Indian possessions', mandarins from the Burmah that Roberts had annexed, Zulu chiefs and headmen from many an African village. Among the fifty thousand troops on parade, the largest

Even the celebrated detective, Mr Sherlock Holmes, is, without his permission, pressed into the service of crude medical salesmanship. An *Illustrated London News* advertisement for 20 January 1894.

number ever seen in London, were the Victoria, the New South Wales and the Queensland Mounted Rifles from Australia, the Gold Coast Hussars, the Bikaner Camel Corps and the Bengal Lancers, the Trinidad Light Infantry, the Royal Niger Constabulary, the British Guiana Police, befezzed Cypriot Zaptichs, white-gaitered Jamaicans and a contingent from Hong Kong in wide Chinese hats. There were the Canadian Mounties and Dyak head-hunters from Borneo, each in a neat red pill-box cap. And there was a twenty-eight-stone Maori from New Zealand.

Military splendour of this sort was only appropriate: this was an era of military pomp and of armies of every kind. Even social work had taken on a quick-step aggressiveness with William Booth naming his East End mission the Salvation Army and teetotalism forming its similar Blue Ribbon Army. ('I was blue ribbon at the time,' the ear-slicing murderer of 'The Adventure

Soldiers of the Queen. The West India Rifles taking part in the Diamond Jubilee parade.

The Salvation Army
in action. A meeting
in the Whitechapel
Road.

of the Cardboard Box' told Holmes during his unexpectedly
moving confession.)

Then, before the Queen left to attend the service at St Paul's,
she visited the Telegraph Room at Buckingham Palace where
she pressed an electric button – this was still the great age of
applied science – and to every corner that was red on the map
there went a message in response to all the telegrams that had
poured in too fast to be opened: 'From my heart I thank my
beloved people.'

A bestseller that year was not a novel, and certainly not a work
on religion, but a book by an Australian author called Fitchett,
Deeds That Won the Empire. And in the music-halls they sang a
new song, 'The Soldiers of the Queen':

And when we say we've always won,
And when they ask us how it's done,
We'll proudly point to every one
Of England's soldiers of the Queen.

But the event was to produce verse of a different colour. It came from Rudyard Kipling, poet of 'The Song of the English'. It was given the title when it was printed in *The Times* of 'Recessional':

If drunk with sight of power, we loose
Wild tongues that have not Thee in awe,
Such boastings as the Gentiles use,
Or lesser breeds without the Law –
Lord God of Hosts, be with us yet,
Lest we forget – lest we forget! ·

The poem spoke to a sentiment that was not dead in England, for all the pomp and shouting. Sir Walter Besant, the novelist, was among the many who wrote to congratulate Kipling. 'You caught the exact feeling – what all decent people with the Puritanic touch in us wanted to have said.'

Sherlock Holmes, English gentleman in the Puritan tradition, once again defeated evil in the 'singular and dangerous web in which our simple Norfolk squire is entangled.' Married to the sprightly American he had met in London, Mr Hilton Cubitt found about a year afterwards that she was receiving curious messages, about which she adamantly refused to speak, made up in the form of lines of little dancing men. But Holmes arrived at Ridling Thorpe Manor too late. Mr Hilton Cubitt had been shot, his wife terribly wounded, possibly by her own hand. Only by deciphering the dancing men code and sending a message in it himself was Holmes able to clear Mrs Cubitt, capture the true criminal and expose, once again, a gang business with its beginnings in lawless, dangerous America.

More cases followed. New battles with the ogre. 'From the years 1894 to 1901 inclusively,' Watson says, 'Mr Sherlock Holmes was a very busy man . . . there were hundreds of private cases, some of them of the most intricate and extraordinary character.' Such a one certainly must have been 'the dreadful business of the Abernetty family' first brought to Holmes's attention by the depth which the parsley had sunk into the butter on a hot day, though we have no details. Two cases only, however, can receive lengthy mention here, one concerned with the worst man in London, the other with the greatest gold-mining magnate in the world.

Rudyard Kipling: caricature by Harry Furniss.

The first case was in essence a simple affair. Holmes was requested by Lady Eva Brackwell, 'the most beautiful *débutante* of last season', due to marry the Earl of Dovercourt within a fortnight, to recover some letters – 'imprudent, Watson, nothing worse' – purchased from a venal servant by Charles Augustus Milverton, 'the king of all blackmailers'. He asked Milverton to visit him, although the man made him feel as one does 'when you stand before the serpents in the Zoo and see the slithery, gliding, venomous creatures'. But the braggart Milverton – 'all because she will not find a beggarly sum which she could get in an hour by turning her diamonds into paste': that is the sort of world Holmes moves in now – calmly refused to budge, even showing the butt of a large revolver projecting from an inside pocket.

So Holmes decided on burglary, swiftly wooing and winning a housemaid in order to reconnoitre the scene. This was not the first time by any means that he had put himself outside or above the law, and it was not to be the last. Such is the privilege of the

'The Area Belle'. It was a housemaid like this that Holmes swiftly wooed as he tackled the case of Charles Augustus Milverton, king of all blackmailers. An illustration from *Living London* edited by George R. Sims, 1902.

Oxford Street, looking towards Oxford Circus: a 1900 photograph. It was in the window of an Oxford Street photographer's that Holmes pointed out to Watson the portrait of the widow of a great nobleman, the lady they had seen shoot Charles Augustus Milverton.

outsider. And of the man of arrogance. But these are heroic qualities, attributes of a superman. What his willingness to adopt the illegal, even his liking for it, also shows is that hidden side of him that always seeks the opposite, the perverse, the dangerous. On this occasion, indeed, that feeling even affected Watson just a little. As, masked, they entered Milverton's large Hampstead house, the staid doctor confessed, 'I thrilled now with a keener zest than I had ever enjoyed when we were defenders of the law instead of its defiers.'

Holmes expertly cracked the blackmail king's safe. But they were soon disturbed by Milverton's unexpected return and had to hide behind his thick, comfort-inducing curtains. There they witnessed a tall, slim, dark, veiled woman come in and empty 'barrel after barrel' of a little gleaming revolver into the blackmailer's body.

It was only later, in the window of a photographer's shop in Oxford Street, that Holmes simply pointed out among the celebrities and beauties of the day a regal and stately lady, and Watson caught his breath as he read underneath her portrait 'the time-honoured title of the great nobleman and statesman whose wife she had been' and who had 'broken his gallant heart and died' when he had learnt through Milverton of her indiscretion – a man of the old school.

Holmes's encounter with the gold king comes in the case Watson called 'The Problem of Thor Bridge', in itself no more than a neat puzzle in detection. Why is the young governess, Miss Violet Dunbar, not the murderer of the millionaire's South American wife? Answer: because, as Holmes proved by noticing a chip in the stonework of the bridge, the passionate lady shot herself and arranged for the pistol to be dragged into the stream, thus seeking to triumph from the grave. But the matter is of more interest for what it shows us about the development by this time of big business.

Neil Gibson, the gold king, had told Holmes, when at last his pride has been humbled ('My professional charges are upon a fixed scale,' Holmes tells him, untruthfully. 'I do not vary them, save when I remit them altogether'), that his business affairs were large beyond the belief of any ordinary man. 'I can make or break – and it is usually break. It wasn't individuals only. It was communities, cities, even nations.'

Money is here a world power. And Holmes sets his face against such a time. 'Mr Neil Gibson', he reflects at the ending of this tragic affair, 'has learned something in that schoolroom of Sorrow where our earthly lessons are taught.'

This, it is worth noting, is one of his few references to religion, though to it we ought to add his declaration in this same affair that 'With the help of the God of justice I will give you a case which will make England ring' and his reflections upon the flowers during the Naval Treaty adventure, already referred to, when he mused a little naughtily, 'There is nothing in which deduction is so necessary as in religion. It can be built up as an exact science by the reasoner. Our highest assurance of the goodness of Providence seems to me to rest in the flowers. All other things, our powers, our desires, our food, are really necessary for our existence in the first instance. But this rose is an extra.' Providence and the God of justice: Holmes, fervid reader of Winwood Reade, that ardent deflator of the claims of established religion, believed only in such a distant Deity. Neither he nor Watson is ever recorded as going to church, enshrined Victorian rule, bar that one occasion when Holmes was conscripted as a witness to Irene Adler's marriage. But he hoped always for some answer from beyond. 'What is the meaning of it, Watson?' he asked at the end of the moving affair of the Cardboard Box. 'What object is served by this circle of misery and violence and fear? It must tend to some end, or else our universe is ruled by chance, which is unthinkable. But what end? There is the great standing perennial problem to which human reason is as far from an answer as ever.' It is the cry of the lost Darwinian.

Holmes's dislike of grossly used wealth can be seen again in the affair of the Priory School, almost the last of his cases we shall look at in any detail. For now he was beginning to envisage bringing his career at last to its conclusion. The prospect of retirement, of laying down his arms with honour in the struggle which he could now see more plainly than ever was bound to be doomed, was becoming more and more welcome.

The world in which he would have to continue his battle was increasingly alien to all that he stood for. There was the dawning new century with its promise of being a different, and worse, era from the one he had come to maturity in. There was the spectacle of the hysterical mafficking that greeted the relief of the besieged town by Lord Roberts's troops – Holmes, Watson tells us, spent 'several days in bed' shortly after the end of the South African War – and there was the death in January 1901 of 'the gracious lady' who had summoned him to Windsor after the business of the Bruce-Partington Plans (while he was engaged in completing his monograph upon the Polyphonic Motets of Lassus) and had there, we understand, presented him with a remarkably fine emerald tie-pin. There was the corresponding advent to the throne of the man who in Holmes's world had imperiously borrowed £50,000 over a week-end and pawned the nation's Beryl Coronet to do so.

The Edwardian Age when, as the American heiress who became Duchess of Marlborough wrote, 'even breakfast, which was served at 9.30 in the dining-room, demanded an elegant costume of velvet or silk. . . . We next changed into tweeds to join the guns for luncheon. . . . An elaborate tea gown was donned for tea, after which we played cards or listened to a Viennese band or to the organ until time to dress for dinner, when we again adorned ourselves in satin, or brocade, with a great display of jewels', was not for Holmes, the man who 'affected a certain quiet primness of dress'. The age that ate at breakfast, as Harold Nicolson the diplomat recalled, 'porridge . . . disposed of negligently. . . . Then would come whiting and omelette and devilled kidneys and little fishy messes in shells. And then tongue and ham and a slice of ptarmigan. And then scones and honey and marmalade. And then a little melon and a nectarine or two' was not for Holmes, the man 'whose diet was usually of the sparest, and his habits . . . simple to the verge of austerity.'

In the early years of that new reign with its swaggeringly rich men, its elaborately elegant and full-blown women, its motor-cars, brassy and blasting, and its luxury yachts, with its open-armed welcome for the heiresses of America and the financiers of central Europe, Holmes's old companion-in-arms married once more and again left the rooms in Baker Street. And at much the same time – 'I remember the date very well,' says Watson, 'the latter end of June, 1902' – there came from Buckingham Palace the offer of a knighthood. Holmes refused it.

It was an action which must seem to us as significant as the large sum of money he did not refuse to accept from – but let us hear Holmes himself reading from one of his often-consulted reference works: '"Holdernesse, sixth Duke, K.G., P.C." – half the alphabet! – "Baron Beverley, Earl of Carston" – dear me, what a list! – "Lord-Lieutenant of Hallamshire since 1900 . . . Lord of the Admiralty, 1872; Chief Secretary of State for –" Well, well, this man is certainly one of the greatest subjects of the Crown!' But plainly Holmes hardly holds him in respect, perhaps because

King Edward VII, the former Royal playboy, with his hosts, the Duke and Duchess of Marlborough, and fellow guests at Blenheim Palace, where even breakfast 'demanded an elegant costume of velvet or silk', at once to be changed in favour of tweeds.

'it was an open secret that the duke's married life had not been a successful one, and . . . had ended in a separation by mutual consent, the duchess taking up her residence in the South of France.'

The beginning of the case in which this great and wealthy subject of the Crown appears, the Priory School affair, was as dramatic as any in all Watson's records. 'I cannot recollect anything more sudden and startling than the first appearance of Dr Thorneycroft Huxtable, M.A., PH.D., etc. His card, which seemed too small to carry the weight of his academic distinctions, preceded him by a few seconds, and then he entered himself – so large, so pompous and so dignified that he was the very embodiment of self-possession and solidity. And yet his first action when the door had closed behind him was to stagger against the table, whence he slipped down upon the floor, and there was that majestic figure prostrate and insensible upon our bearskin hearthrug.'

Dr Huxtable, author of *Huxtable's Sidelights on Horace* – Latin, the language of the stern Roman (and of Catullus) was still entrenched in Britain's schools – had lost the most cherished pupil in his preparatory establishment, the Duke of Holdernesse's only son. 'His Grace has already intimated that a cheque for five thousand pounds will be handed over to the person who can tell him where his son is, and another thousand

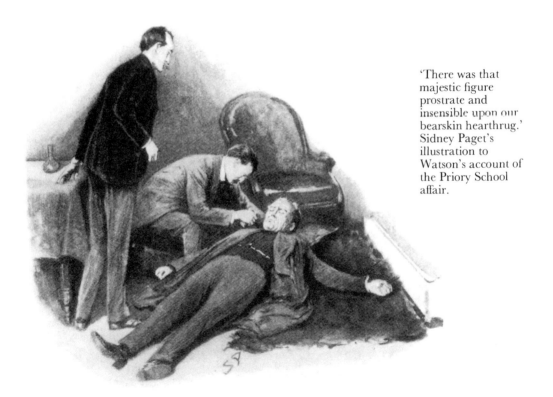

'There was that majestic figure prostrate and insensible upon our bearskin hearthrug.' Sidney Paget's illustration to Watson's account of the Priory School affair.

The Duke of Holdernesse with his young private secretary, James Wilder, beside him as they confront Sherlock Holmes.

to him who can name the man, or men, who have taken him.' And this, remember, when a pensioned-off Army doctor could live in London on 11s. 6d. a day, a mere £200 a year. No wonder Holmes murmured, 'A princely offer.' And we may well suspect the prince he had in his sharply cutting mind was that free-spending former Prince of Wales.

The three of them set off to the school 'in the cold, bracing atmosphere of the Peak country', though note that in another case in these late days, the Shoscombe Old Place affair, when Holmes also had occasion to castigate an aristocrat who had failed to behave with decency, we hear for the first time of central heating, eventual doom of spartan England. At the Priory School they found the Duke, with beside him his young private secretary, James Wilder, who generally saved him the trouble of direct address.

'You are well aware, Dr Huxtable, that His Grace is particularly anxious to avoid all public scandal. He prefers to take as few people as possible into his confidence.'

The browbeaten headmaster suggested at once that Holmes returned to London by the morning train.

'Hardly that, Doctor, hardly that,' Holmes said, at his blandest. 'This northern air is invigorating and pleasant, so I propose to spend a few days upon the moors, and to occupy my mind as best I may.'

At this the Duke himself invited Holmes to near-by Holdernesse Hall.

'I thank your Grace. For the purposes of my investigation I think that it would be wiser for me to remain at the scene of the mystery.'

It is the Duke's opinion, we learn, that his son has fled to his mother 'aided and abetted by this German'. This German is Herr Heidegger, the language master for these ten- and twelve-year-olds, who has also disappeared with his bicycle. Yet another instance of the German influence in the Britain of that day.

'By a singular and happy chance,' as Watson puts it, both the roads leading away from the school were under observation on the night of the boy's disappearance, and so Holmes is led to the moors stretching away behind the grounds. Day was just breaking next morning when he woke his partner, much as he had done in the Abbey Grange affair when he had cried, 'Come, Watson, come! The game is afoot!'   ·

Here it is 'Now, Watson, there is cocoa ready in the next room. I must beg you to hurry, for we have a great day before us.'

Soon they found wheel tracks. 'A bicycle certainly,' Holmes said, 'but not *the* bicycle. I am familiar with forty-two different impressions left by tyres. This, as you may perceive, is a Dunlop, with a patch upon the outer cover. Heidegger's tyres were Palmers.' But before long they had hit on Heidegger's tracks, though almost immediately after they found gorse 'all dabbled with crimson'.

'Bad!' said Holmes. 'Bad! Stand clear, Watson! Not an unnecessary footstep! What do I read here? He fell wounded, he stood up, he remounted, he proceeded. But there is no other track. Cattle on this side-path. He was surely not gored by a bull? Impossible! But I see no traces of anyone else.'

And in a minute or two more they found the body of the German master.

James Wilder, pedalling for dear life, is watched by Holmes and Watson from their hiding-place.

Holmes deduced that since he had left 'without his socks' he had pursued the boy who must too have been on a bicycle, otherwise the German would not have needed his. But the German had been killed 'by a savage blow dealt by a vigorous arm', not by a mere boy. Yet nowhere were there any traces of a man.

'Holmes,' Watson cried, 'this is impossible.'

'Admirable! A most illuminating remark. It *is* impossible as I state it, and therefore I must in some respect have stated it wrong.'

The Dunlop track led them by evening to the far side of the moors where it might equally, over harder ground, have gone on to Holdernesse Hall or to a wretched inn. While they were near this latter they saw James Wilder, the secretary, come hurrying along to it on his bicycle. Holmes contrived to examine the machine's tyres, chuckling to find the rear one a patched Dunlop. Soon it occurred to him how he must have stated his facts at the murder scene wrongly. There had been no cattle about, so the tracks he had seen must have been made in some other manner, probably from their characteristic pattern by a horse. 'What a blind beetle I have been.'

Next day Holmes presented himself at Holdernesse Hall, chillingly insisting on seeing the Duke even if in bed and, once confronting him, suggesting he could speak more freely in James Wilder's absence.

'The fact is, your Grace, that my colleague, Dr Watson, and myself had an assurance from Dr Huxtable that a reward had been offered in this case. I should like to have this confirmed from your own lips.'

The Duke confirmed it. 'My friend,' the naïve Watson writes, 'rubbed his thin hands together with an appearance of avidity which was a surprise to me, who knew his frugal tastes.'

'I fancy I see your Grace's cheque-book upon the table,' Holmes continues. 'I should be glad if you would make me out a cheque for six thousand pounds. It would be as well, perhaps, for you to cross it. The Capital and Counties Bank, Oxford Street, are my agents.'

The Duke's beard turned more aggressively red than ever against his ghastly white face.

'And whom do you accuse?'

'I accuse *you*,' said Sherlock Holmes.

It turns out that James Wilder is the Duke's loved illegitimate son, who has discovered the secret of his birth and presumed 'upon his power of provoking a scandal'. Now he has kidnapped the heir, still held captive, hoping to force the Duke to break the entail on his huge estates, though his plan had gone wrong when the brave Heidegger had started in pursuit and been killed by the rascally local innkeeper.

Scornfully Holmes thrust aside the Duke's offer to double the £6,000 in return for complete silence. 'To humour your guilty elder son you have exposed your innocent younger son to imminent and unnecessary danger. It was a most unjustifiable action.'

He speaks for the world he used to know. The world where an English gentleman, however great, however humble, behaved always with decency.

'The proud lord of Holdernesse was not accustomed to be so rated in his own ducal hall,' Watson tells us. 'The blood flushed into his high forehead, but his conscience held him dumb.'

There is a little tail-note to the story. Holmes asks the Duke whether it was from his illegitimate son that the murderer learnt the dodge of disguising a horse's tracks as those of cattle. The Duke shows him a set of iron trick shoes used by the marauding Barons of Holdernesse in the Middle Ages.

'Thank you,' Holmes says. 'It is the second most interesting object that I have seen in the North.'

'And the first?'

Holmes, Watson says, folded up his cheque and placed it carefully in his notebook. 'I am a poor man,' he added, as he patted it affectionately and thrust it into the depths of his inner pocket. We can see the action as a final implacable gesture of rebuke to the coming times.

But Holmes would have a good use for so large a sum. Within two and a half years of that day he had bought himself a small farm on the Sussex Downs where he could devote himself to bee-keeping and study. There were not a few cases in the intervening period, including the affair of the Illustrious Client already discussed and the matter of the Three Garridebs in which Watson received a revolver wound and heard his unemotional friend say, 'You're not hurt, Watson? For God's sake, say that you are not hurt.' It was worth a wound, Watson tells us, 'it was worth many wounds to know the depth of loyalty and love which lay behind that cold mask.'

But now Watson has married again and his records are fewer, nor do any of the cases he does deal with merit particular attention. There was to be one more astonishing flare-up of the still-powerful Holmes fire, and another small flicker, but the long fight was at last finished. Holmes had not conquered in it. He never could have done. But he had laid down his arms, bloody but unbowed.

His helmet now shall make a hive for bees.

Amid the brash vulgarities of the Edwardian Age Sherlock Holmes lived in retirement. But his life's work was not yet quite done. He seems never to have completed the textbook that would focus the whole art of detection into one volume which he had threatened in Watson's Abbey Grange narrative, though he did produce a *Practical Handbook of Bee Culture, with some Observations upon the Segregation of the Queen.* Chance, too, put in his way the matter of the Lion's Mane, with a body on the very beach nearest his home.

Yet there was also one more grave task he was asked to perform for his country. Even this he was reluctant to take up.

He had striven mightily in a mighty battle and it had gone
against him. Little wonder he was unwilling to buckle on again
the stiff armour. 'The Foreign Minister alone I could have
withstood,' he said to Watson when it was all over. 'But when the
Premier also deigned to visit my humble roof . . .'.

What the Prime Minister had asked Holmes to do was to
identify and checkmate a master spy for the Germany that had
been year by year moving more clearly into direct opposition to
Great Britain. As early as 1896 the Kaiser had telegraphed
President Kruger congratulating him on repelling the unofficial
attempt by Dr Jameson to annex the Transvaal, in many ways
the high point of aggressive British Imperialism. There had

The shadow of the
Great War ahead.
An *Illustrated London
News* artist depicts
sailors making a 25-
knot torpedo-boat
destroyer ready for
action.

King and Kaiser in deadly
rivalry: a German
cartoonist's view.

been, too, the juvenile rivalry between King and Kaiser, with
Edward, it is said, creating the Kaiser a field-marshal for Queen
Victoria's funeral because he knew that he himself looked much
the better in uniform. Then in the years from 1902 onwards
Britain's leaders had felt compelled to abandon the policy of
'splendid isolation', seen at its height at the time of the Second
Stain adventure when it was put to Holmes that the country
must not be tipped by popular indignation into either of
Europe's two armed camps, and they had entered into treaties of
mutual assistance with Japan, with France, with Russia. From
about 1908 onwards Germany's throwing of her resources into
her navy was another visible threat, and Britain responded by
building new capital ships. 'The Admiralty had demanded six,'
Winston Churchill wrote, 'the economists offered four: and we
finally compromised on eight.'

The Times, 2 August 1914, 'the most terrible August in the history of the world.' Two days later Great Britain joined the conflict.

To perform his task Holmes went into hiding, crossing the Atlantic, changing his name, growing a little Uncle Sam goatee, joining an Irish secret society in Chicago – shades of the Dancing Men and the Scowrers or Molly Maguires – and over two whole years establishing himself as a virulent anti-Briton, going so far, back across the Atlantic again, as to give 'serious trouble to the constabulary at Skibbereen'. In this way he was recommended at last to the master spy, one Von Bork, who, though secretly responsible for 'half the mischief in England', had won his way into British society to the point of being spoken of as 'quite a decent fellow for a German' by boxing, playing polo, drinking hard and taking prizes for his four-in-hand at the Olympia horse shows. He was a man who had always contrived, as his confidant

Benz automobile of 1912–14. In such a car, symbolic of a new age, Baron von Herder came to visit the spy-master, Von Bork, at his coastal residence.

at the beginning of the narrative, the diplomat Baron Von Herling had not, to appear to keep the rules of 'good form', that mysterious code they acknowledge as still fundamentally governing life in England.

The two of them discuss in this conversation – it takes place on the night of 2 August 1914, 'the most terrible August in the history of the world' – whether in a day or two they will have to leave if war is declared. Von Herling thinks Britain may let France and Belgium face the German armies alone. 'She would at least have peace for the moment.'

'But her honour?'

'Tut, my dear sir. We live in a utilitarian age. Honour is a medieval conception.' And they had besides 'stirred up such a devil's brew of Irish civil war, window-breaking Furies, and God knows what to keep her thoughts at home.'

The two stare out across the sea where the setting sun has left 'one blood-red gash like an open wound' in the distant west. In the sultry and stagnant air there is 'an awesome hush and a feeling of vague expectancy' so that, our narrator tells us, 'one might have thought already that God's curse hung heavy over a degenerate world.'

It was chiefly to gloat over the boiling-point conflict in Ireland between Protestant, Union-supporting North and largely Catholic, English-hating South and over the activities of the Suffragettes as well over the easily exploitable greed of the master spy's sub-agents that Baron Von Herling has come here in his 100-horsepower Benz car, symbol of a new age, a very different age from the days when Holmes and Watson went by dog-cart or wagonette over the unmade-up country roads, dusty white or red or muddy yellow. Von Bork was waiting only for the last of the stolen secrets he had bought, the key to Britain's inexplicably changed naval codes. He confidently expected next day to come slipping in with them at the little door on the Duke of York's Steps, the confidential side-entrance to the German Embassy. They were to be brought to him that very evening by a renegade Irish-American who 'seems to have declared war on the King's English as well as the English King', one Altamont.

Soon after Von Herling had gone the man arrived. But Von Bork, of course, was in for a shock. When he opened the packet of new naval codes he found instead a small blue book with printed across its cover in gold letters *Practical Handbook of Bee Culture* and the next moment 'he was gripped at the back of his neck by a grasp of iron, and a chloroformed sponge was held in front of his writhing face.'

In a few moments 'Altamont' is joined by the man who has driven him (in a small Ford) to the rendezvous, and Holmes and Watson are together again mulling over points of interest in yet another affair. And, as they escort Von Bork to the car, Holmes points to the moonlit sea and shakes his head thoughtfully.

'There is an east wind coming, Watson.'

'I think not, Holmes. It is very warm.'

'Good old Watson! You are the one fixed point in a changing age. There's an east wind coming all the same, such a wind as never blew on England yet. It will be cold and bitter, Watson, and a good many of us may wither before its blast. But it's God's own wind none the less, and a cleaner, better, stronger land will lie in the sunshine when the storm has cleared.'

We do not know whether Holmes lived long enough to see how that hope-charged prophecy fared. The sole remaining record we have of him comes from Watson's preface to the volume which concludes with that final adventure. Some years later Watson did put before the public a few more accounts of earlier cases, not without a warning that any further attempts on the dispatch box 'with my name John H. Watson, M.D., Late Indian Army, painted upon the lid' in the vaults of the bank of Cox and Co., Charing Cross – a bank destroyed by enemy action during the 1939–45 War – would be countered by the publication of 'the whole story concerning the politician, the lighthouse and the trained cormorant.' And there were other accounts, we know, like that concerning the ship *Matilda Briggs* and the giant rat of Sumatra, 'for which the world is not yet prepared'.

But the only authentic record left to us of the world's first and greatest consulting detective comes in these words of his faithful Boswell's published in 1917: 'The friends of Mr Sherlock Holmes will be glad to learn that he is still alive and well, though somewhat crippled by occasional attacks of rheumatism.'

The rest is silence.

List of Illustrations

Index